REMARKABLE REPRINTS

A COLLECTION OF ACCLAIMED ARTICLES & CROWD-PLEASING COLUMNS

DARLENE HOUSE

REMARKABLE REPRINTS:
A COLLECTION OF ACCLAIMED ARTICLES & CROWD-PLEASING COLUMNS

©2009 Darlene House

Published by G Publishing LLC
P. O. Box 24374
Detroit, MI 48224
www.juliathepublisher.com

Printed in the USA.

Library of Congress Control Number: 2009901242

ISBN 13: 978-0-9823533-4-9
　　　 10: 0-9823533-4-0

FOR EVERYONE WHO
ALLOWED ME TO HELP
TELL THEIR STORY AND
THE PEOPLE THAT THEY
WERE ABLE TO INSPIRE

EXPRESSIONS OF GRATITUDE

Heartfelt Thanks To:

*Sam Logan (***Michigan Chronicle/ The Michigan FrontPage***) for being a newspaper industry pioneer plus supporting original publication and reprint of articles/columns.

*Karen A. Love (***Michigan Chronicle/ The Michigan FrontPage***) for supporting original publication and reprint of articles/columns. I am also grateful for Karen A. Love's thought-provoking contribution shared in "Views from Community News Leaders (VFCNL) – Part I.".

*Margaret Lewis (***Legacy/ Legacy News***) for supporting efforts related to the original publication/reprint of articles/columns. I am also grateful for Margaret Lewis' enlightening contribution shared in "VFCNL – Part II.".

*My other editors/publishers who supported all of the efforts related to the original publication/reprint of contents. They are: Carolyne Blount (***about...time magazine***), Denise Crittendon (***African American Family***), Jennifer Kluge (***Corp!***), Joann Loveless (***The Aurora***), Sue Voyles (***Corp!***), and the teams at the Warren/Center Line/Sterling Heights Chamber of Commerce (*The Exchange*).

*Francis Datillo (City Comix/Stellar Scholars) for suggesting I meet/introducing me to some of the aforementioned editors/publishers plus creating column heads for some of my work. I also appreciate all of the support and encouragement you have given me since we first met during our advertising agency days.

*Julia Hunter (G Publishing LLC) for providing encouragement to complete this project and supporting me during an extended, challenging post car accident recovery time. You helped this book to evolve from a dream into a reality and quality product.

*Sylvia Hubbard (Hub Books/Motown Writers Network) for being my "Internet Guru" and encouraging me to publish a book as well as helping others to promote their books. Your efforts have helped my Internet presence to evolve for three important entities – namely House of Communications, National Inspirational Role Models Month and *REMARKABLE REPRINTS*.

ADDITIONAL ACKNOWLEDGEMENTS

An achievement such as the publication of this book was not possible without the support and contributions of many people. I will mention some of them here but the list is not all inclusive of everyone who has affected the project. Rest assured that I am definitely grateful to everyone for everything.

*Almighty God for always making a way out of no way plus being the ultimate source of my strength and divine inspiration.

*My maternal Grandmother Louisiana Hines. At 111 years young, you are still my ultimate inspirational role model. Thank you for allowing me to visit "Casa de Louisiana" whenever I needed a nearby work retreat site.

*My mother and best friend, Allean H. House. The life you lived made me value education and aspire to achieve great things. Thank you for your unconditional support.

*My brother and advocate, David L. House, Jr. Through the years, you have become a cherished friend and favorite critic. Your insights help me to strive hard to achieve my personal best and produce quality products plus provide first-rate client services.

*All of my other family members and friends. You have touched my life in so many ways with your cherished love and support.

*Every teacher/trainer who taught me the essential skills, answered my many questions and encouraged me to seek out new truths.

*All of my mentors and mentees. Thank you for the priceless lessons and treasured moments shared with each other.

*Hartford Memorial Baptist Church pastors, ministers and members for your prayers and support down through the years from my early days as a "Hartford Baby" until now.

*Women in Communications of Detroit members for support in identifying and contacting article/column subjects, project support, creative collaborations and encouragement.

*Detroit Working Writers members for your expert insights and encouragement. I also appreciate that you were willing to share your resources and contacts with me plus enhance my projects/events with your skills, talents and presence.

*All of my professional colleagues for your generous assistance and enthusiasm for participating in collaborations.

*Sigma Gamma Rho Sorority, Inc. members who showed me the true meaning of sisterhood in an infinite number of ways.

*All of my article/column subjects. I am eternally grateful for the fact that you shared your stories with me. It was a cherished honor for me to share news about you with others.

*My responsive readers. The fact that I heard from you made it clear there are still people who appreciate the printed word in newspapers and magazines. Read on!

IMPORTANT
DEFINITIONS*

Remarkable

Notably or conspicuously unusual,
extraordinary.
Worthy of notice or attention.

Reprint

1. Something that has been printed
   again.

*The American Heritage Dictionary of
English Language, Fourth Edition*

AUTHOR'S NOTE:

Due to the fact that most of the contents of this book are reprints, some of the contact information for people or resources featured in the articles or columns may have changed since original publication date. If you experience some unsuccessful communication attempts and need assistance reaching any of the featured entities, you can contact the author. Assistance will be provided if deemed appropriate based on specific people or resources you wish to contact.

INTRODUCTION

It is a wonderful blessing to have had the opportunity to meet, interview and write about hundreds of people. Every single one of them had interesting stories to tell. I have enjoyed sharing their diverse backgrounds, experiences, achievements, missions and ministries with readers throughout the world.

This book grants the request of many of my readers, editors and publishers. They wanted me to create a collection of my work. In these pages, you will find some of "my greatest hits" among the articles and columns published in distinctive magazines and newspapers distributed throughout the world. My brother, David L. House, Jr. suggested the criteria selection focus. The articles and columns reprinted here earned strong reader responses, critical acclaim or rave reviews.

The people, businesses, organizations, places and things featured as my article/column subjects truly reflect diversity. I have always been interested in history. Thus, it is no coincidence that historical links and reflections are often highlighted in my work. It is my hope that you will enjoy getting to know my article/column subjects. From the current second-oldest Detroit citizen on record featured in the first article who has always been a significant part of my life to the diverse people I encountered throughout the years, it was truly amazing to see how the different article/column subjects enlightened and inspired me.

Writing for decades has truly been a labor of love. When I was in high school, it was thrilling to have my first articles and poems published in professional publications. God willing, my final articles and poems won't be published for many years to come because there are still many more stories that I want to tell. I hope that you enjoy this "greatest hits" collection. Based on the feedback I have already received, anticipations call for this book to be the first in a series.

VIEWS FROM
COMMUNITY NEWS LEADERS
(VFCNL)

Featuring Contributors

Karen A. Love
Publisher, *The Michigan FrontPage (MFP)*
COO, *Michigan Chronicle/MFP*
1st Vice Chairwoman
NNPA – Black Press of America

and

Margaret D. Lewis
Publisher/Editor
Legacy News

VFCNL PART I.

For decades, our publications provided a significant public forum. That's why our slogan – "Voice of the Community Since 1936" – means more than those powerful words can say. We have taken them seriously as a call to service.

It is undoubtedly true that many of the people featured in *Michigan Chronicle* would not have been spotlighted elsewhere. They are minorities and others making important contributions frequently over-looked or taken for granted by their contemporaries. We have shared their stories gaining recognition and support for them.

The achievements of our younger generations are also deemed newsworthy and shared via *The Michigan FrontPage*. They needed a publication to applaud their achievements and milestones while show-casing their diversity. Our recent evolution of the publication reflects its quest to uniquely serve its audiences.

Darlene House has written for both of our publications. Several of those articles and columns appear in this publication. One of our esteemed columnists, Marie Teasley, featured Darlene as a young woman on the rise. She has definitely risen to the occasion when writing for us. Her work reflects a shared love of history and commitment to community service.

There has been substantial debate about the future of newspapers. Community newspapers must adapt for modern times but they still play an important role among print media. As the articles reprinted in these pages show, community newspapers often function as griots by sharing stories linked to our heritage. They also reveal our dreams and aspirations. Whether you're sitting back in an easy chair or scrolling down a computer screen, time spent reading community newspapers can always be a rewarding experience.

Karen A. Love
Publisher, *The Michigan FrontPage (MFP)*
COO, *Michigan Chronicle/MFP*
1st Vice Chairwoman
NNPA – Black Press of America

VFCNL – Part II.

Ten years ago, in 1999, I discovered that the town I live in did not have a community newspaper. Due to working two jobs all of my adult life, I hadn't found time to notice that there was not a written source of news and information of concern to townsfolk. When I wanted to inform property owners of a lawsuit that could directly affect how the city charged them for water service, I saw the need for a newspaper for our town.

Providing information and local news is a big responsibility. Writing is a very specialized craft. Although I had worked with words as a court reporter for many years, I knew that more was needed in order to publish information and news in such a critical area as a community newspaper. I was and am eternally grateful to have had the counsel and services of Darlene House in the creation and continuation of the *Legacy News* community newspaper.

Legacy News is a newspaper based in Highland Park, Michigan, which features articles about the Woodward corridor,

Michigan's only American Scenic Byway Urban Road. Darlene shares my appreciation for the history linked to this exceptional road. In these pages, you will find some of her columns written for the "Michigan Roads" and other series that she originated. They reflect a special ability to make historical facts and revelations interesting.

Darlene has helped in every aspect of the presentation of news and information from the time of creating **Legacy News**, formerly known as **The Legacy**, to the present. Frank Dattilo, artist/owner of City Comix and Stellar Scholars visionary, introduced me to Darlene. They have both been valued guides during my journey to provide news and information to enlighten, strengthen and empower readers.

With this effort, Darlene has taken another step in her service to provide material readers will find both valuable and enlightening. Reading her writings will greatly enrich your life and I consider it a privilege to be included in her work.

Margaret D. Lewis
Publisher/Editor
Legacy News

*RE*MARKABLE
*RE*PRINTS

TABLE OF CONTENTS

*RE*MARKABLE *RE*PRINTS

CHAPTER ONE

POSITIVE PROFILES

Centenarian Reflects On Women's History Month

When she was seven years old, Alabama native Louisiana Hines yearned to get a close-up look at an "amazing automobile". Then, one day, it happened.

"They didn't have paved roads back then," recalls the Detroit centenarian. "I hoped a car would get stuck in the sand near my house, and finally it did. That was the shiniest, black beautiful thing I had ever seen in my life."

The car, which Hines and other children ran out to see, was a Ford Model T.

She took a long look while Black men assisted the young White man driving the car. Back then, cars coasted down hills but struggled to climb them.

That's the way things were in those days, according to Hines. She should know. Next month, she will celebrate her 107th birthday. The fifth oldest Detroiter, Hines was featured in two chapters of *If I Live to be 100: Lessons from the Centenarians*. Written by Neenah Ellis, it is a companion book for the National Public Radio Series "One Hundred Years of Stories." She also was honored at Mayor Kwame Kilpatrick's 2004 centenarian birthday party.

"It's exciting and a blessing to see how many things have changed since I was a child," says Hines, who still lives alone and does all of her own cooking, and cleaning. She spends her days making crafts from discarded items, memorizing poems to recite at special events and occasionally designing and sewing clothes for family and friends.

Born April 13, 1898, Hines grew up with minimal education during a time, she says, when children and women were seen, not heard.

"If you didn't know your place, they would put you in it, so next time no one was confused," she explains. She became a farmer's wife, but after raising two sons and a daughter, she and her husband Arthur Hines pursued other opportunities. She managed a restaurant, assisted bakers, and provided child and elderly care services before the couple migrated up North to realize another dream: Her husband wanted to work in the auto industry.

Detroit exceeded her expectations. "When I got off the bus, there were the tallest buildings I had ever seen, and cars everywhere," Hines says.

Overall, there were more opportunities as well. Hines enjoyed working as a "Rosie the Riveter" in an airplane plant, while her husband worked at the Packard automotive plant. After earning a beauty culture license at Bee Dew Beauty College, Hines owned and operated the L. Hines' Beauty Shop in Detroit. As for her longevity, she doesn't know the secret but thanks God that a prophecy made by her mother has been fulfilled.

"An obedient child would live a long life."

*This article first appeared in **African American Family** magazine in March 2005 and is reprinted with permission.*

Issuing a Clarion Call
Former Journalist Strives to Unite Community Through Nonprofit

Luther Keith believes its time for a true Detroit renaissance. The former award-winning editor and columnist for *The Detroit News* urges everyone to "be part of the change" by working together to improve the quality of life for children and families. Keith's brainchild, ARISE Detroit!, issued that "clarion call" in June 2005.

"ARISE Detroit! is a voluntary movement," explained Paul Riser, Jr., the coalition's 2nd vice chair and Legacy Associates Foundation founding member. ARISE is an acronym for Activating Resources and Inspiring Service and Empowerment.

"This kind of movement is not going to be accomplished overnight," Riser acknowledged. "I have been pleased with the direction and energy ARISE has brought to Detroit."

Since its founding, ARISE Detroit! (www.arise-detroit.org) grew from 22 founding partners to a coalition of more than 180. "Those 22 founding organizations were chosen because they wanted to come together under one unified banner," Riser points out.

Before retiring from *The Detroit News* in 2005, Keith interviewed many people and wrote hundreds of stories about issues related to children and families. He had stints as a sports writer, state capitol correspondent, city editor, state editor, business editor, assistant managing editor, public editor and columnist. Keith frequently developed and coordinated stories/special reports addressing quality of life issues affecting Detroit.

"We had enough organizations but there were not enough people involved in trying to fix things and we needed to find a way to get more people involved," the native Detroiter says.

Through the years, Keith was a visionary leader and enthusiastic volunteer. In 1985, he took a leave of absence to become founding director of Wayne State University's Journalism Institute for Minorities, which provided recruitment and training for media careers. Keith also served as vice-president for the National Association of Black Journalists. His avid support of community events, such as the annual Metro Detroit

Youth Day, has made him a familiar face in the community.

"Luther's connection to the community has been an asset to ARISE because it has opened doors to have conversations with a lot of individuals," says John X. Miller, ARISE Detroit! chair of steering committee and Detroit Newspaper Partnership director of community affairs. "Luther has been able to go in and make some meaningful program initiatives work throughout Detroit."

Keith proudly notes that ARISE Detroit! has mobilized more than 1,000 volunteers and secured Skillman Foundation funding through 2008. "I consider working with ARISE Detroit! a logical extension of the many issues I wrestled with as a journalist," he adds.

As executive director of ARISE Detroit!, Keith stresses the importance of being team players so everyone can get in the game to be part of the solution. "I focus on getting buy ins and win wins," he explains. "My goal is what can I do to help you do a better job and get the word out."

Keith's ability to consistently think like a newspaper editor and effectively utilize the media is a priceless asset. He is grateful for the support of others who realize the importance of journalists having a conscious and reaching out to their community while media works with everyone to transform it.

ARISE Detroit! also benefited from celebrity support. "While traveling around the country, Bill Cosby had positive things to say about us," Keith says.

John Miller says the organization has definite promise.

"ARISE Detroit! is in its infancy but we realize there is a tremendous amount of promise and work ahead and Luther is the person to get us there".

This article first appeared in **Corp!** *magazine in June 2007 and is reprinted with permission.*

Governor's Press Secretary Manages Communication Flow

Governor Jennifer M. Granholm's Press Secretary Elizabeth D. Boyd is a "consummate professional" who discovered working in state government was a "total fit".

Boyd shared insights about her career and experiences working with "probably the coolest public official" during the, Women in Communications (WIC) of Detroit March meeting. She was inducted as an honorary member of the professional organization that champions the advancement of women across all communications disciplines. For additional information about WIC, call (248) 652-1460.

Although she didn't work on our first female governor's campaign, Boyd was excited about the vision of what Granholm could bring to the office.

Granholm appointed Boyd to be her press secretary in December 2002. Prior to that, Boyd served as communications director for Michigan Secretary of State Candace C. Miller and her long serving predecessor Richard H. Austin. As a graduate of Michigan State University with journalism and advertising degrees, she used her knowledge and skills effectively to earn recognition among other professionals. The award-winning communicator was actually recommended for her position by a majority of the Lansing press corp.

Reflecting on working with some of Michigan's outstanding political leaders, Boyd takes pride in the accomplishments. There is not a lot of time for pensive moments, however, due to the fast pace of her current work setting.

"It is only in the past couple of months that my head doesn't spin," Boyd confessed. She is still in awe of the amount of work and number of projects handled by the Governor's office. A typical day includes early morning senior staff meetings followed by responding to media inquiries and frequently traveling to public appearances before preparing briefing notes keeping everyone up to date.

"Our first year was challenging because we were laying the ground work," Boyd observed. "No matter how bad a situation is, she [the Governor] wants to find the good in it." Boyd added that our energetic leader has shown exceptional communication skills in challenging times such as during the Benton Harbor crisis and the blackout.

Boyd also acknowledged that Granholm has become "a player on the national scene" resulting in more national media attention. She appeared on such diverse shows as the Saturday Today Show and Real Time with Bill Maher.

"The challenge for me is to keep up with the issues," Boyd admitted. "I don't even pretend to say that we know about all the issues." She believes it is extremely important to get all of the information to assist reporters and make sure to say the right thing by having the best information.

As a busy wife of an insurance agent, Boyd knows a key to ongoing success is pacing. Life lessons taught the importance of realizing when you are doing too much and adjusting accordingly. Boyd is a Lansing native who has managed to have an amazing career in her hometown.

"As long as the Governor will have me and I can keep up, I'll be there," Boyd promised. Based on her past achievements, that's a promise she is destined to keep.

*This article first appeared in **The Michigan FrontPage** in December 26, 2003 issue and is reprinted with permission.*

Senator Jackie Vaughn III.
Leaves Inspiring Legacy

Senator Jackie Vaughn III. resolved to bring the achievements of unsung heroes and heroines to the attention of others. Before his death on September 12, 2006, Vaughn touched many lives.

Born on November 17, 1917 in Birmingham, Alabama, Vaughn was the seventh child of nine children born to William and Myrtle Vaughn. He graduated with honors and the highest distinction from many schools including Highland Park Community College, Oberlin College and Oxford University. Vaughn became a Fulbright Scholar and Fellow at Oxford.

"His outstanding education fueled his service," said Michigan Lt. Governor John Cherry. "He believed it was a gift he wanted to share with others." Cherry credited Vaughn with being a champion for education and young voters. Vaughn's legislation created the Michigan Virtual University making it possible for people in rural areas to obtain a quality higher education.

Vaughn was also applauded for being a civil rights champion. He led recognition efforts for Dr. Martin Luther King, Jr. and strongly supported sanctions against South Africa along with apartheid.

In his role as a deacon and Sunday School teacher, Vaughn distinguished himself among other Hartford Memorial Baptist Church members. He held the Contemporary Issues Sunday School Class together for more than 30 years. The class was renamed to the Jackie Vaughn III. Contemporary Issues Sunday School Class in honor of its esteemed late teacher.

"If he said he was going to do something, he did it," said former Sunday School class member and political campaign worker Willa Clark. "He was a wonderful person who helped my family many times."

During my undergraduate years at Michigan State University, he was a tremendous help to me, too. It was difficult for me to find a suitable internship until Vaughn welcomed me into his office family. As he had with others, Vaughn shared insights about why he was so driven to create and distribute resolutions. They were much more than cherished keepsakes highlighting life achievements. The resolutions also recorded in the historical archives of our state enlightening information that could be read for years to come.

In the years after my graduation, we often talked about other lessons Vaughn taught me. Notable among them was "the skill of enacting 'charismatic cameos' ". Throughout his terms as a state representative and senator, Vaughn consistently maintained an intense schedule working in Lansing during the week and returning to his home district on weekends. On several occasions, he showed me a schedule for the day that was jam-packed with events. Vaughn had a charming way of cordially making his presence known upon arrival, handling business efficiently and graciously departing for the next stop.

"He was a master of the art of efficiently giving public recognition," said former Harlem Globetrotter and Black Legends of Professional Basketball Foundation President Dr. John L Kline.

Vaughn's last stop will undoubtedly be a heavenly resting place. Wouldn't it be great if all of the dearly departed people he had given resolutions to were there to greet him? Winter, Spring, Summer or Fall, in spite of the weather, all you had to do was call on him. Vaughn would do his best to be there. Hartford Memorial Baptist Church pastor and Vaughn's eulogist Rev. Dr. Charles G. Adams acknowledged that his dear friend "believed he had no right to rise unless he was dedicated to lifting others in the climb". Let's keep his inspiring legacy alive by climbing on and reaching back to help others along the way.

*This article first appeared in **Legacy News** in October 1 – November 4, 2006 issue and is reprinted with permission.*

*RE*MARKABLE
*RE*PRINTS

CHAPTER TWO

EMPOWERING PEOPLE

Holbrook Cares for Homeless

Colleen Holbrook wants everyone to take a closer look at the homeless.

"When most people see them on the street, they run away," she said. "If you get to know them like I have, it changes your viewpoint."

As a community liaison representative for Mercy Primary Center, a continuing ministry of Trinity Health, Holbrook cares for homeless people.

"They all have a story to tell and do not all come from dysfunctional families," she said. "Many of them are former professionals and valued contributors to the community that now treats them like strangers."

Holbrook often reflects on one of her favorite Scriptures for inspiration.

"And the King shall answer and say unto them, 'Verily I say unto you, in as much as ye have done it unto one of the least of these my brethren, ye have done it unto me'." (Matthew 25:40 KJV)

Mercy Primary Care Center, located at 5555 Conner Ave., serves uninsured adults and provides a critical access point for health care services. Trinity Health commits $2 million annually to support related efforts.

There are 12 exam rooms and transportation is available. The center celebrated its second anniversary on March 12 and has served approximately 2,300 patients since opening its doors. Holbrook said people without insurance leave with what they need.

Uninsured adults often live below the poverty level. Chronic health conditions such as diabetes, hypertension, cancer, asthma and other untreated illnesses exist at an alarming rate. The center's services include primary medical care, basic radiology, mammography, laboratory services, prevention and health education, pharmacy services and pharmacy patient assistance program.

"What we do here is a ministry and it ministers to us, too," Holbrook said.

She is proud of her Specialized Personal Assistance (SPA) program. It is designed to provide individuals and their immediate family members with quality donated clothing plus shower access and personal hygiene items. She knows that homeless people cannot just wash their cares away. Yet, she has seen the difference improving appearances makes in improving attitudes and building self-esteem.

Holbrook believes the Mercy ministry is unique because it addresses the body, soul and spirit.

"Christ was practical," she said. "He didn't always give out fish and bread. People were taught how to fish themselves; just as we try to help others turn their lives around."

Holbrook enjoys working with a dedicated team that reflects sincere concern for others.

When Holbrook was a Providence Hospital practice manager, it was center team member Dr. Margaret Meyers who shared her vision to help the under-insured and under-served. She did not immediately follow Myers to Mercy. Approximately two years later, the former director of The Crisis Pregnacy Center of Detroit joined her. Holbrook was concerned about spending enough time with her son and daughter.

"I love being out there serving," she said. "I do not like just sitting behind a desk."

She interacts regularly with community leaders. They are contacted regarding how helping the population she serves can be mutually beneficial. A spring clothing drive encouraged people to donate specific items due to limited storage space.

"Most of our homeless people are men," Holbrook noted. "We accept gently-used items in good condition but only give out new name brand underwear."

Holbrook finds it rewarding when her efforts are appreciated.

"Our clients not only thank me, they help others by volunteering," she said. "When I get discouraged, they cheer me up."

Holbrook admitted it is sometimes extremely difficult to find housing for homeless people with limited incomes. There are very few rooming houses left and some of her homeless people only make $35 per day throwing leaflets.

Holbrook remembers growing up in New Jersey with a father who "let life allow him to make excuses and feel sorry for himself". When not drinking, he was a great person. He died young, but Holbrook was raised by a strong mother and grandmother.

After reflecting on personal experiences, Holbrook stated that some homeless people visiting the center think they can never go home again.

"I tell them you can take all of this and let it be a springboard for a new life, plus be hope and help to someone else. Many people come here feeling down and out but leave feeling good about themselves."

For additional information about the center and its services, call (313) 579-4005.

This article first appeared in **Michigan Chronicle** *"Women of Purpose" section in July 28 – Aug. 3, 2004 and is reprinted with permission.*

African Art Appreciation 101

Catherine C. Blackwell's African art appreciation is evident when she shares her collection and wisdom with others.

The retired educator fell in love with African art and started collecting items during her first visit to the continent.

.   "I thought it would be a wonderful way to introduce history and culture to my students," said Blackwell.

She had discovered perceptions of Africa were far removed from reality. "The major incentive for my first trip to Africa was to let children know what it was really like," she explained. "Images came from Edgar Rice Burroughs' made-up version of Tarzan, but I found a warm and loving people on that continent."

Blackwell traveled to Africa 65 times, frequently accompanied by students/teachers for trips up to six days long. The largest group consisted of 85 people from throughout the United States who visited four African countries.

"My goal is to take students from Blackwell School to East Africa where they can stay with Kenyan families," said the namesake of Detroit's Catherine C. Blackwell

Institute of International Studies, Commerce and Technology, plus the Catherine C. Blackwell African Collection.

More than 650 items have been catalogued for Blackwell's collection. It has been estimated there are at least 600 more items. The overall theme is things children would enjoy. Item categories include toys made by African children, masks, musical instruments, clothes, children's books and African American collector's editions. Some books, awarded from her great uncle Charles Sheldon's collection are treasured collector's items.

Blackwell placed items in cases and took them to schools and public events. She enjoyed seeing children's smiles when they put the clothes on and heard stories about the chief or king who wore them.

"I wanted them to feel like a chief and king, too," she said.

Although Blackwell still schedules public appearances, she charges fees that are donated to the Catherine C. Blackwell Scholarship Fund established with retirement party gift proceeds.

Due to the related expenses, Blackwell didn't set out to collect large museum pieces.

Her diverse collection has attracted the attention of experts. A beaded throne from Nigeria was donated to a Newark museum at the curator's request. Additional donations will be made to an impressive list of sites including the Detroit Public Schools' African Heritage Museum, Children's Museum and the Museum of African American History.

The Detroit Public Library, which previously gave her the Whitney M. Young Award, recently spotlighted items from her collection in its brochures announcing special events.

Blackwell's advice to potential African art collectors is to ask yourself whether you like it. "It may not be a great work of art but it can have value to you," she said.

Blackwell cautions everyone to be careful about checking for authenticity.

"You have to be observant and make sure items weren't made in China – especially when buying clothes," she warns. "Efforts by others to copy African art reflect the attraction of its beauty and design."

At press time, details were being confirmed for an April Scarab Club event. The format will be similar to Public TV's popular traveling antique show. For details about this

Blackwell collection fundraiser, call 313-863-7832.

*This article first appeared in **The Michigan FrontPage** in February 22, 2002 issue as part of the "Revelations" series and is reprinted with permission.*

In Tune with Deaf Community and Troubled Children

In school, Dr. Marietta Alston learned to hear things differently and grow stronger. A music teacher told her she was tone deaf. Alston sang in the Cass Technical High School Gospel Choir, Donald Vails Voices of Deliverance, Rejoice Community Choir and New Vision Gospel Choir. Her family provided inspiration and support. Her grandmother played the piano. Her mother was a lyric soprano who studied at Wilberforce University and performed throughout Michigan.

All but one of the nine children in Alston's family took piano lessons. Her father piled his children and neighbors' kids into a station wagon for trips to the Detroit Institute of Arts and symphony.

Until last winter, Alston spent every year of her life except one living in the Detroit westside neighborhood where she was raised by "the village".

The only living immediate family member, Michael Malik Alston, is a gifted musician/singer/writer/painter. Alston wants to play the piano and sing like her baby brother. "I still enjoy singing but don't do solos," she revealed. "When I am signing and interpreting solos, that is my way of singing them."

While signing at Hart Plaza events and the Million Women March, Alston found her comfort zone. She had felt compelled to take Hartford Memorial Baptist Church signing classes that changed her life.

Alston laughed about literally being dragged down her church's center aisle the first time she was scheduled to sign for a service. Thanks to her teacher and mentor, Reichelle "Pam" Anderson, she copied the right signs. Afterward, she accepted her calling by listening to and serving special populations.

Reflecting back, Alston remembers writing a paper about working with hearing parents of deaf children during her first year at Wayne State University.

"Ninety percent of all deaf individuals are born into hearing families and ninety percent of the families do not learn sign language, leaving these individuals isolated," said Alston who wanted to be a pediatrician but did not like math.

A counselor pointed out, she was eligible for concurrent degrees in psychology and sociology.

Anderson, founder and CEO Deaf Options, introduced Alston to the Center for Humanistic Studies where she earned a clinical and humanistic psychology M.A. plus humanistic, clinical and education psychology specialist degrees. Approximately 10 years were spent at Deaf Options.

Assignments included therapy and outreach in homes plus supporting keeping deaf children at home. Lessons learned for The Union Institute doctorate of philosophy graduate involved adapting tools and being flexible.

"It was rewarding to see smiles on deaf people's faces when they found new ways to communicate." Alston recalled about the close-knit community.

She advised aspiring clinicians and signers to become actively involved in the deaf community and really get to know the unique culture/population. Doing this made it easier to work in mainstreaming situations such as when Alston assisted a hearing impaired social worker with becoming her sister in Sigma Gamma Rho Sorority, Inc. – Rho Sigma Chapter. Alston was also one of the first women in Michigan to work with deaf and hearing impaired people who experienced violence.

Through the years, Alston has worked with many other special populations including mentally challenged youth ages 12 – 17.

"When meeting new clients, I tell them we're on a journey and the trip is within you," she said. "My job is to point out the highlights and bring them up later when you are ready to deal with them," said the Black Family Development therapist and psychologist. Alston is also a certified addictions counselor, level one.

Alston plans to start more deaf ministries such as the one at Kadish Baptist Church.

Everyone is invited there for Praise in Motion on Sept. 13 at 6 p.m., featuring dancing and signing with deaf and hearing groups from throughout metropolitan Detroit.

Alston also collaborated on a three-tier workshop series for women at Kadesh and wants to work with others creating targeted services.

"Church is a place of healing tormented souls and can be a total healing place if leaders listen well, then step up to provide counseling services to the congre-gation," she said.

*This article first appeared in **The Michigan FrontPage** in September 12, 2003 issue and is reprinted with permission.*

You Can Go Home Again Financial Pro Concludes

When she was 8, Glinda F. Bridgforth decided to always be in control of her money and life. Adventures along the way made that tougher than she had anticipated it would be.

"Let's face it: Often we have to hit bottom, be broken down and humbled before we're able to let go of old destructive beliefs and patterns and rebuild our lives on a healthy, solid foundation," she wrote in her acclaimed book, *Girl, Get Your Money Straight! A Sister's Guide to Healing Your Bank Account and Funding Your Dreams in 7 Simple Steps*.

This book is a practical guide selected as one of the Detroit Public Library's African-American Booklist 2002 adult top 10 picks. Its publication marked Bridgforth's 25th year as a financial professional.

Looking back over the years, Bridgforth can see how life experiences were all part of a divine plan. The native Detroiter was raised in a family of six children without a real concept of wealth. Although she enjoyed math, she doesn't remember anyone ever suggesting that a financial career be considered as an option. Before being hired by a major

California bank, valuable experience was gained while still a Western Michigan University student through working at the credit union and Detroit Bank & Trust.

She tells stories about living in "virtual prosperity" to maintain an image of success. Reckless spending led to $50,000 in unsecured debt. After leaving a demanding job and failed marriage, she was able to tune into a holistic approach.

The founding of Bridgforth Financial Management Group addresses the "close link between how we view ourselves in relation to money and how effectively we manage our lives". Her entrepreneurial practice of the last 13 years has focused on teaching others life altering lessons and self nurturing skills. Bridgforth advises everyone to question traditional definitions of success.

With a consistent client base of 50 percent African American and 50 percent Caucasian, Bridgforth was initially encouraged to write a general audience book. Publisher feedback led to targeting for an African American female niche.

Positive feedback and reviews resulted in planning for a "Girl" franchise. Titles are linked to Bridgforth's mother's melodic "Hey, girl" greeting in long distance calls to

Oakland, CA. The second series book, *Girl, Make Your Money Grow: A Sister's Guide to Expanding Your Wealth and Enriching Your Life*, was co-authored with local stockbroker Gail Perry-Mason. This collaboration served as a model for future efforts and yielded new ideas to assist broader audiences with expanded resources.

Both Bridgforth's collaborative and solo efforts are guided by the following principles. 1) Maya Angelou's quote, "Easy reading is hard writing." 2) "Am I really saying what I want to say?"

Bridgforth's views about traveling regularly back to the west coast changed after experiencing Sept. 11 travel delays and related challenges. After settling back into Motor City living, she found you really can enjoy coming home again.

This article first appeared in **Michigan Chronicle** *and* **The Michigan FrontPage** *"Women of Purpose" Special Commemorative Edition in May 7-13, 2003 and is reprinted with permission.*

*RE*MARKABLE *RE*PRINTS

CHAPTER THREE

CREATIVE PEOPLE

Prolific Poet Laureate

"My selection as poet laureate was not something I sought," said Naomi Long Madgett when she appeared as the featured speaker at a Rotary Club breakfast. In April 2001, Detroit Mayor Dennis Archer appointed this tremendously talented woman to a four-year term. She follows the city's first poet laureate, Dudley Randall who was appointed by Detroit Mayor Coleman Young and served until his death.

Like Randall, Madgett has inspired many others. "I had an influence on a number of poets who achieved success locally and nationally," Madgett stated. "I am very happy to have been a stepping stone for people who might not have gotten a start as early as I did."

Madgett got off to a very early start by having her first volume of poetry published when she was 17 years old. To date, she has published eight volumes of poetry that have been highly anthologized and used in textbooks. One of my favorites is her award-winning *Octavia and Other Poems*, which eloquently reflects the quest for family history.

In 1972, while she was a full professor in the Department of English and Literature at Eastern Michigan University, this prolific poet found time to found Lotus Press. That press has enjoyed 29 years of dependable, uninterrupted service and the publication of more than 80 titles, many of which are still in print. After news spread about Madgett's publishing activities, she received manuscripts from throughout the world. Her highly-acclaimed 20th anniversary anthology, **Adam of Ife: Black Women in Praise of Black Men**, represents a timely breakthrough in the way the African American male is viewed, especially by African American women.

Each year, Lotus Press sponsors The Annual Naomi Long Madgett Poetry Award. The winning author of a book-length poetry manuscript receives $500 in cash and his/her work is published and distributed. Past winners include acclaimed poet Bill Harris in 1999 for his **Yardbird Suite, Side One: 1920 – 1940.**

Madgett would not be surprised if the poetry collections mentioned here did not appear on your reading list.

"Most people do not read or buy the books," she acknowledged. "If a book of poetry sells 800 copies, it is said to have done well." Madgett and other poets face the unfortunate reality that "although poetry relates significantly to the experience of every culture in the world, it does not enjoy a popular audience in this country."

As poet laureate, Madgett views herself as a representative for all artists. She explained that the term laureate has been used since the 15th century and relates to ancient Greeks who placed laurels on winners' heads. A woman who uniquely combines creativity and vision, Madgett has high standards for her genre. "I want poetry that has literary excellence and the ability to stand the test of time," she proclaimed. Mayor Archer asked Madgett to write a special poem commemorating Detroit's 300th birthday for inclusion in the time capsule. She will undoubtedly be inspired to create another timeless masterpiece.

*This article first appeared in **The Legacy** in July 2001 issue as part of "Highlights and Insights" series and is reprinted with permission.*

Author's Dream: Motivate Dreamers

Debra B. Darvick knows that achieving your dreams can make a dramatic difference in many lives. One of her biggest dreams was to become a published author. Darvick's critically-acclaimed book, *This Jewish Life: Stories of Discovery, Connection and Joy*, shares many stories reflecting people pursuing their dreams and those who succeeded in reaching them. One of my favorites among the book's 52 stories shares experiences of a talented urban architect who became the inspired designer of a holy tabernacle.

"Your dreams take you into uncharted territory" is one of the 7 teachings for following your dreams that Darvick reveals in public presentations. On Thursday, January 11, 2007, she will be the featured speaker during the Local Author Book Fair in the Southfield Public Library Meeting Room at 7 p.m.

"We have 4 Local Author Book Fairs a year and we are showcasing authors from the community," said Jane Sloan, from the Southfield Public Library Community Outreach Department. "It gives them an opportunity to meet other authors and readers."

Like many other talented authors throughout the Metropolitan Detroit area, Darvick enjoys spending time with people who love words. She acquired an enhanced appreciation for words growing up in a family where both parents were wordsmiths.

"Books are more than just paper for anyone who loves to read," observed Darvick. Although originally conceived for Jews who had good experiences and something to say, readers have found *This Jewish Life* to be universal. "We learn through stories," Darvick said. "The Bible is a storybook and the Torah is a layered study of words," Darvick cherishes stories about her grandfather, Abe Berkowitz. He was a civil rights lawyer who "made history and was a part of it". Berkowitz supported Dr. Martin Luther King, Jr. Darvick fondly remembers reading her grandpa's letters including one from Robert Kennedy. "Letters allow you to touch what the person touched and see their hand-writing," Darvick stated.

As a self-described "writer who beads" and makes beautiful jewelry, Darvick earned praises for diverse expressions of creativity. She has instructed others in making bracelets with yoga words. Her articles were published in widely read mainstream and

Jewish publications. Darvick earned several awards for her work. She was two-time recipient of Simon Rockower Award given by the American Jewish Press Association for Excellence in Jewish Journalism. Darvick also was the three-time recipient of Detroit Working Writers Award of Excellence/ Nonfiction.

The Birmingham resident is proudest of being the mother of two young adults. She encourages them and others to pursue their dreams. "The teaching of dreams is a creative way of sharing the experience of writing the book," Darvick revealed. "There are lessons that can apply to anything." For additional information about Darvick or to order her book, visit debradarvick.com.

This article first appeared in **Legacy News** *in January 7 – February 3, 2007 and is reprinted with permission.*

Cadences of Glory and Gratitude Celebrates Clifton and All States Anniversaries

Music has the ability to transcend barriers of geography, language, class, gender and race. During the past five decades, African-American Pianist Edith Clifton has delighted audiences with her performances in concert and recital throughout the United States, Canada and Europe.

Appearances included solo recitals in New York at Carnegie Recital Hall and Lincoln Center Performing Arts Library; Paris at the American Cultural Center and on French National Television. Upon completing a European concert tour, Clifton was soloist with the New World Symphony Orchestra at Avery Fisher Hall, Lincoln Center.

After many years as a resident of New York City, she returned to Detroit, playing a solo recital at the Interlochen Arts Festival and, after auditioning with Music Director, Gunther Herbig, she performed the Schumann Piano Concerto with the Detroit Symphony Orchestra.

Native Detroiter Clifton began her music studies with Doris Tarver and the

Detroit Public Schools. More serious study commenced at the Detroit Conservatory of Music where she studied with Gizi Szanto. Studies continued at Wayne State University where she won several awards including the Sigma Alpha Iota Scholarship. In 1955, she won the nationwide piano competition of the National Association of Negro Musicians. She moved to New York City and continued her studies as a scholarship student of Alton Jones of the Juilliard School of Music and Madame Olga Stroumillo. During the last decades, Clifton has coached exclusively with Jeaneane Dowis.

Since earning a Master of Arts degree in 1978 from the New School University in New York, Edith has enjoyed a dual career as a video producer/director and media consultant in New York, New Jersey and Michigan. Her list of clients has included Black Legends of Professional Basketball Foundation (BLPBF).

"Edith Clifton created a dynamic video that I am still proud to show during public events," said Dr. John L. Kline, BLPBF Founder and President, and a Cadences of Glory and Gratitude Honorary Co-Chair. "She is a multi-talented individual and captivating concert pianist."

Clifton has also earned critical acclaim. "Edith Clifton's account of the solo part of Schumann's Piano Concerto was a successful one...A most persuasive bit of work," reported the *New York Times* regarding orchestral debut. Related to recital debut, the *Times* acknowledged Clifton is "...a serious, sensitive artist [with] rhythmic vitality and bravura".

Gazzettino, Pordonone, Italy said, "The pianist demonstrated her artistic sensitivity and exciting musicality".

Legacy News is proud to be a media sponsor for *Cadences of Glory and Gratitude*. The Sunday, December 4, 2005 event also celebrates the 63rd anniversary of the sponsoring group, Hartford Memorial Baptist Church's All States Club Ministry. That group unites people from diverse geographic areas in the spirit of Christian love and unity that transcends all boundaries.

Cadences of Glory and Gratitude features a 2 p.m. Pre-Concert Strolling Dinner in Hartford's Fellowship Hall followed by a 4 p.m. Concert with Edith Clifton and special guest. Concert only tickets are $10 and packages range from $15 - $30 including dinner/CD/DVD options.

For additional information or ticket/package/commemorative items orders call 313.255.6274.

This article first appeared in **Legacy News** *in November 2005 issue and is reprinted with permission.*

Keir Shares Keys To Success

Native Detroiter Keir (key-air) believes the best way to survive a lay off is to prepare for the life changing experience before it happens. That is what he did while working as a supervisor and industrial engineer for a "Big Three" automotive company. Keir earned a B.S. in Engineering from Michigan State University but went back to school. He learned how to become a recording engineer and start a business. Consequentially, Keir gained an enhanced appreciation for what it takes to be successful while "working in a business based on what you love to do and are passionate about".

Keir frequently falls back on the experiences gained while working in corporate America. "My industrial engineering side assists me in running my business and keeping costs down with as little waste as possible," he explained. "It helps me to balance my creative side by using everything I learned including time management skills."

Word to the wise, before you step out on your own, try to save some money. Keir recommends that amount equal or exceed what you earn working for others. Then, becoming an entrepreneur won't cramp your style. Keir also recommends that you obtain as much education as possible while still employed by a company. It will be beneficial in the long run even if you have to work overtime.

Keir has learned many important lessons both inside and outside the classroom. At the beginning of this year, he spent approximately $170 dollars on books. Many of them were autobiographies. He recalls inspiring aspects of the life stories of fellow African American men Johnson Publishing Company pioneer the late James Johnson and film director Spike Lee.

"I thought if they could do it, I can do it, too," Keir revealed. Like the legends he read about, Keir became a risk taker. "My own drive to be successful and finding ways to solve problems along with God's help opened doors for me," he acknowledged.

Although Keir appeared at Bakers Keyboard Lounge and many poetry sites, he doesn't just sit back waiting for the next gig. Audiences at events where Keir was featured, including Java & Jazz and Detroit Festival of the Arts, experienced his empowering energy.

Through Lord and Jackson Sound-wave Productions, Keir produced his "No Need to Worry" CD. It is a high-quality professionally mastered CD featuring narrative poetry, lyric poetry and music all written by Keir. The music behind the poetry is a "fusion" of jazz and gospel hip hop. His goal is to put listeners' in a "better state of mind" considering all of the negative things happening in the world today. Topics creatively addressed in an uplifting manner include unemployment, facing layoffs, worries, hard times or just having a bad day.

"My music is done the old fashioned way, one instrument at a time without sampling or loops," explained Keir. "Literally 100% of the people had positive feedback and said that they enjoyed the CD." The writer of this article was definitely one of them. In fact, after listening to the CD, one doesn't question Keir's belief that his business is capable of tremendous growth. He looks forward to producing some "smokin' slam in' stuff" for other artists one day. Keir would also like to do more work with businesses creating distinctive music for their jingles and Web sites.

As a successful workshop leader, Keir wants to schedule more interactive sessions focusing on a variety of topics including poetry writing and popular "What to look for in a Mate" presentations.

At press time, Keir was scheduling a tentative August appearance at Soul Day. He was also hard at work refining his next CD scheduled for an early 2007 release. There are on line opportunities to obtain more information about Keir or order his "No Need to Worry" CD at www.sonicbids.com or cdbaby.com/keir2 respectively. Both amateur and professional critics are encouraged to listen to tracks and share their feedback on line. Keir can be reached at creativesoundwaves@yahoo.com.

This article was previously published in **Legacy News** *in 2006 and is reprinted with permission.*

*RE*MARKABLE
*RE*PRINTS

CHAPTER FOUR

TREASURED
RESOURCES

Wise Widows Share Wisdom

Whether a husband's death is expected or sudden, it has a dramatic impact on the wife left behind. She must carry on in a world that frequently misunderstands her.

"Where do I fit in? I thank God for this group because it was prayed into existence," said a woman at the Widows With Wisdom (WWW) Launch Luncheon in September. It was the brainchild of another widow, Minister Mary Darlene Edwards.

Edwards, co-founder of Joy of Jesus along with the late Rev. Eddie K. Edwards, envisioned WWW before becoming eligible for membership. In February, she reflected upon meeting three widow friends and felt the need for a related support ministry.

Edwards was destined to experience more than empathy. Rev. Edwards fought cancer for five months and passed in July. His widow saw first hand what it meant to endure weeping for a night followed by joy in the morning.

"God prepared me and I know the peace of God so I am in a grace bubble right now," Edwards revealed. Although she never saw herself burying her husband, Edwards has coped with her loss in many ways that defy depressed-woman-wearing-only-black stereo-types and benefit others. She found strength to carry on as founder/leader of The Called and Ready Writers, a Christian writers group, and His Lovely Wife Ministries. The acclaimed author of **Ponderings from the Heart of Mary** and journalist shared her story with others while adjusting to life without her best friend.

Edwards considers herself to be a blessed woman for many reasons. She still cherishes memories of her husband but also looks forward to the future. That is understandable considering her status as the only Detroit contributor published in the new bestseller **Chicken Soup for the African-American Soul.** Edwards also offered editorial assistance for the book featuring her revealing story "Excuse Me, Who's Just Another Statistic?" about being an unwed mother at 13.

Widows and people with a desire to assist them confirmed the need for WWW. The mission is "to educate, encourage, and embrace those who must learn how to make the adjustment to living without spouses". Pastors have admitted that their church ministries lack the support and resources in this area. There is a void in the types of widely available support groups when it comes to spiritually-based ones specifically targeted at widows.

WWW Program Director Dessie Morgan offered the following suggestions for recent widows spending the first holiday season alone. Spend some quality time with family and friends. A memorial dinner could also allow everyone to reflect on the holiday season and the joyous occasions experienced with your mate. Each person could tell something funny or interesting about the dearly departed and the gifts he gave everyone. Overall, focus on the good times that everyone shared together.

WWW meets the first Saturday of each month from 1 to 3 p.m. Widows of all ages are encouraged to participate and share their experiences and insights. Call (248) 663-2363 for additional information. You can also e-mail mwwinc@aol.com or holyfamily@angelspace.com.

*This article first appeared in **Legacy News** in November 7 – December 4, 2004 and is reprinted with permission.*

Enterprising Women Meet At Local Museum

"Enterprising Women: 250 Years of American Business" finally gives outstanding leaders some of the recognition they deserve. The Detroit Historical Museum is the only Midwestern and the final stop for a national touring exhibition showcased through Saturday, January 9, 2005. It marks the first time major themes of women's history have been woven into the American business story.

These amazing women and their lives, challenges, and achievements are portrayed through artifacts, costumes, diaries, business/legal documents, photographs, paper items, moving images and interactive video portraits. The impressive list includes two women with Detroit connections: Pewabic Pottery Founder Mary Chase Stratton and Brownie Wise, who developed the Tupperware party concept.

In conjunction with the national exhibit, a local companion exhibit called "With Style and Service: Detroit's Enterprising Women" features six historic and influential businesswomen and community leaders. They include dress shop owner Louise Nobyn D'Haene, department store founders Lora Pack and Francis Wolin, cosmetic school proprietor/hair care product inventor Vivian Nash Hill, custom fashion designer Ruth Joyce, and one other distinctive woman.

For the ladies of Sigma Gamma Rho Sorority, Inc.'s Rho Sigma Chapter, proud hostesses of the well-attended November multi-generational "family/friends" group tour, Rosa Slade Gragg was especially notable among the local honorees. An esteemed Rho Sigma Chapter co-founder and past Basileus (president) Gragg was also an acclaimed civic and civil rights leader. She was appointed to positions by and served as advisor for three presidents: FDR, Kennedy and Johnson. Gragg founded the Slade-Gragg Academy of Practical Arts in 1947. It was the first African American owned and operated business on Detroit's main street, Woodward Avenue. "If there ever was a woman who could fit the description of the ultimate nurturer, seemingly born with the strength to lead and to seize the opportunity, it was Rosa Lee Slade Gragg," proclaimed a panel in the exhibit showcase. The following Gragg quote supports that statement: "We cannot advance depending on other people; we must build up an economic responsibility for ourselves." Those words are reflective of pearls of wisdom humbly shared by Gragg with people of all ages, including me.

One of the wise docents for the Rho Sigma tour, Ken Laws, believes it is important for youths to experience history. His sons, Kenneth L and Jared Laws, worked as youth volunteers. "I see this as a great experience allowing kids to get exposures working with adults and other kids while learning about history and the city of Detroit," Laws said.

"It is a neat program and they keep coming back for more so I guess it can't be all bad," said Eleanor Austin, co-advisor, along with Janet Salaminen, for the 41 young volunteers ages 12 – 17. They are given the creative freedom to plan their own projects, work with projects for all Detroit Historical Society sites, become gallery guides and assist with cultural center special events. Austin acknowledged parent support has contributed greatly to the program's success.

"Many people who have never visited the Museum need to come and see us," said Guest Relations Assistant Stephanie Moss. She pointed out there are also a lot of innovations for returning visitors to discover. "It is my job to make your visit enjoyable to encourage you to visit us again," Moss said.

Anyone visiting the Museum during Tupperware Weekend, December 11 and 12, is encouraged to donate a piece of Tupperware and earn a half price admission discount. The Tupperware containers will be donated to Gleaners Community Food Bank for use in boxes that will be distributed to needy families this holiday season.

For additional information about Enterprising Women or the Detroit Historical Museum and its projects, visit www.enterprisingwomenexhibit.org or call 313.833-1805.

*This article first appeared in **Legacy News** in January 2 – February 5, 2005 issue and is reprinted with permission.*

Civil Rights Museum Provides Unforgettable Journey

During a recent trip to a major metropolis on the Mississippi River, I traveled back in time to gain historical insights. The National Civil Rights Museum in Memphis, TN, told stories in ways never experienced before.

For this history buff, it was an unforgettable journey revealing truths others denied or refused to share.

My quest for knowledge led to the museum site housed in the Lorraine Motel site of the assassination of Dr. Martin Luther King, Jr. After the events of April 4, 1968, the small minority-owned business in the south end of downtown Memphis gained notoriety.

The motel's owner, Walter Lane Bailey, kept a couple of rooms as a shrine to his wife and King. Loraine Bailey died of a brain hemorrhage two hours after the civil rights leader was shot.

Prominent Memphians saved the foreclosed property from destruction as a result of actions taken by their Martin Luther King Memorial Foundation. In December 1982, the foundation purchased the Lorraine at auction for $144,000. With support from local and state government entities, funds were raised to create and construct a civil rights center. The National Civil Rights Museum opened its doors on Sept. 28, 1991.

In 2002, the museum opened a $11 million dollar expansion called "Exploring the Legacy" with exhibits covering civil and human rights movements to 2000, plus evidence surrounding the investigation of King's assassination.

My first and last impressions of the original museum building involved viewing the balcony outside Room 306 where King was assassinated and a replica of the room as it was that infamous day.

Along the way, there were many more moving experiences. Opting to spend more than my travel guide's estimated one hour and half minimum, the recorded guided tour led by Ossie Davis and Ruby Dee was frequently paused.

My journey followed a timeline featuring photos, artifacts, exhibits, dioramas, models, replicas, videos and tape recordings.

At one point, I explained how a group of children on a community center field trip could participate in a "wheel of fortune-like" interactive exhibit. The wheel shared common excuses Blacks heard when denied the opportunity for voter registration. One youngster said, "After all that, I will never forget to vote for somebody or something." Out of the mouths of babes.

Speaking of youth, some of the most memorable exhibits dealt with the plight of youngsters involved in the civil rights movement. They included the cell with a row of uncomfortable beds for children.

Another moving sight was the diorama featuring footage filmed in front of Little Rock's (Arkansas) Central High School when nine Black students tried to enroll there.

Such scenes and many others throughout the site aroused many emotions including anger, sadness, pride and joy. For information about The National Civil Rights Museum visit www.civilrightsmuseum.org or call 901-521-9699.

*This article first appeared in **The Michigan FrontPage** in August 20, 2004 issue and is reprinted with permission.*

Curtis Museum Celebrates Carver History

"The love that has gone into this project is irreplaceable," said Mary Jones, president of Mary Jones and Associates, and longtime protégé of Dr. Austin W. Curtis. As the third link in the legacy started by Dr. George Washington Carver, Jones takes pride in the new Curtis Museum honoring its namesake and mentor.

"It is a wonderful celebration of the legacy for Dr. Curtis and Dr. Carver to be honored here," acknowledged Jones.

The Curtis Museum spreads throughout the House of Beauty (HOB) Hair Mall west wing at 14022 W. McNichols in Detroit.

"Everything here has a history to it," Jones explained.

True collector's items include letters from Carver to Curtis, photos with other history makers, selected volumes from the Curtis library and items used for experiments. There is also a music room reflecting the diverse musical collection Curtis enjoyed sharing with family and friends.

When Curtis moved to California last year, artifacts were left in the custody of HOB owners Douglas and Christine Crawford. The

Crawfords spent countless hours preserving and displaying the treasures buried in bags and boxes.

"It is my dream to relocate the museum to the Curtis Laboratories site located on Selden," Crawford said.

In the meantime, metropolitan Detroiters have an opportunity to visit a site where everyone can learn more about great African American scientists.

"People who came through our doors as the museum evolved were amazed," said Jones, a chemist and corrective hair specialist trained by Curtis. They enjoyed evidence of great African American contributions found in some history books but frequently left out of others.

Born in slavery in January 1864, Carver had a dramatic impact on agriculture in the South. He taught farmers about planting crops along with cotton subject to destruction by the boll weevil beetle. The crops included peanuts, soybeans and sweet potatoes. Carver invented hundreds of products related to those crops. The visionary genius made it possible for us to have products commonly used today such as cheese, mayonnaise, peanut butter, shampoo, sugar and shoe polish.

Before his death on Jan. 10, 1943, Carver trained his successor. Curtis, also affectionately called "Baby Carver", worked with his mentor at Tuskegee Institute. Lessons Curtis learned resulted in the creation of hair care and beauty products.

During his years in Detroit, Curtis supported community awareness events such as Carver Day hosted by Sigma Gamma Rho Sorority, Inc.-Rho Sigma Chapter at Curtis Museum on Jan. 19.

"Dr. Curtis generously shared his time and wisdom with school children and adults," acknowledged event chair and retired Inkster Public Schools educator Allean H. House. The past Rho Sigma Basileus (president) met Carver while he was working in his Tuskegee laboratory during a childhood trip with her mother. Curtis became an admired friend she invited to speak at schools and public events including Northland Shopping Center forum.

"Curtis carried on the work of a great man and made significant contributions of his own through an impressive comprehension of ways to apply science," House said.

Curtis Museum tours can be scheduled by calling Jones at 313-341-1513.

"We welcome everyone who is interested in experiencing history," said Jones.

*This article first appeared in **The Michigan FrontPage** in February 7, 2003 issue and is reprinted with permission.*

*RE*MARKABLE *RE*PRINTS

CHAPTER FIVE

IMAGINATIVE INVENTIONS

Playing for Success
Board Games Enhance Business Skills

'Tis the season for fun and games. We just celebrated National Game and Puzzle Week (November 23 – 29, 1997) and games are always popular selections for holiday gift-giving. The quantity and variety of board games can keep relaxing business people from being bored this winter. Playing board games has been a great American pastime since they were introduced in the 1800's. In addition to the classic board games, avid players are turning to modern alternatives for fun ways to spend their leisure time. Join *The Exchange* for a look at some perennial favorites and new innovations that can enhance business awareness and skills.

Created in 1955 by James Brown Cooke, The Original Careers® Game lets players make decisions about what career paths to experience. Diverse selections include computer programming, ecology, entertainment and space exploration. Experiences and opportunities help players earn fame, fortune and happiness.

Participants in the Michigan State University and University of Michigan alumni rivalry can continue their school-spirited fun by playing Spartanopoly and Michiganopoly. These games are one of the many customized editions of Monopoly®, the popular real estate trading game. Others include the Harley-Davidson®, Heirloom and Star Wars™ Classic Trilogy editions. If you have a great idea for a special edition, remember official versions require licensing from Parker Brothers and they only work with toy companies. Late for the Sky Production obtained special permission to create many editions inspired by major university campus areas.

TV-opoly™ is the media mogul game endorsed by *TV Guide*. It allows players to compete in negotiations involving newspapers, magazines and TV shows to become the most successful strategic expert. Featured TV shows range from classics such as "I Love Lucy" to today's "Friends" trendsetter. The winner must have more money, higher rated shows and awards acclaim than other players.

If you've turned green with envy watching Tiger Woods and other golf pros, Fore™ is the game for you. You can start on the first hole and continue until all nine holes have been played. The player finishing with the fewest strokes wins. Improving your golf board game skills can help you to stand out on the real course. Maybe next year you'll be a prize winner at the Chamber's annual golf outing.

When you're looking for unique games, don't forget to check the selections offered by small companies. One of *Games Magazine*'s Top 100 games for 1997 comes from Propel, Inc. Propel, a Detroit-based game manufacturer, just introduced CLUCHE. This game features over 1,000 of America's favorite cliches. Andre Williams designed the game that lets players work as teams while exercising their verbal skills.

Whether you win or lose, playing games with business themes can be fun ways to challenge your mind and skills. So, pick a classic or modern board game. Roll the dice. Spin the wheel. Draw a card. Whatever the final scores are, you will have experiences that are both educational and entertaining while spending quality time with family and friends.

*This article first appeared in **The Exchange** in December 1997 issue.*

Woodward Celebrates 90th Anniversary

On the first chilly day of August, a special celebration warmed our hearts. It was a time to take pride in the nine-decade legacy of a road we often take for granted.

As reported in the August *Legacy*, 1909 became a major milestone when the first mile of concrete road was laid on Woodward between Six and Seven Mile Roads. That particular section of Woodward was probably selected because this location marked where the county's jurisdiction began. It also was an important area because Ford's new Model T plant, down the road in Highland Park, would be turning out a large number of new automobiles.

Inspired by Ohio and Windsor (Canada) success stories, where there were concrete applications for sidewalks and alleys, road commissioners Edward Hines and John Haggerty decided the time was right to test concrete on a major thoroughfare.

Other rougher surfaces had been used for paved roads including brick, cobblestone, and macadam. Brick and cobblestone were uneven and labor intensive. Macadam consisted of stones sprayed with tar to form a wear resistant surface that didn't last long.

"It's not an overstatement to say that this mile of road changed the course of history," said Wayne County Executive Ed McNamara. "Without a smooth, reliable road to move traffic, the success of the new automotive industry was far from guaranteed. Once Wayne County filled that need with this concrete road, the sky was the limit for Henry Ford and the rest of the automobile industry," McNamara explained.

As a featured anniversary celebration speaker, McNamara shared an interesting historical fact about Ford. Henry Ford served as the Wayne County Road Commissioner in 1906 but declined extended service to avoid a conflict of interest.

The anniversary celebration crowd gathered early on the afternoon of August 19 near the Woodward historical marker in Palmer Park. They were treated to Stroh's ice cream and Vernor's ginger ale. Exhibits featured recently discovered photographs of the actual street paving. Other event high-lights included singing "Happy Birthday" with a barber shop quartet and watching vintage automobiles cruise down Woodward.

We know Woodward Avenue is destined to have many more special celebrations in the future. There will be great opportunities for enhanced recognition now that Woodward is a Michigan Heritage Route eligible for funding to highlight its history.

Remember to keep turning to *The Legacy* for more news in our series of articles about our wonderful Woodward Avenue and other special Michigan roads.

More First Mile of Concrete Highway Facts

Opening Day:	July 1, 1909
Length:	1.2 miles
Width:	24 feet
Thickness:	6 ½ inches
Cost:	$13,492.83
Worker's Pay Examples:	
	Foreman: $3 per day
	Engineer: $3 per day
	Laborer: $1.80 per day

*This article first appeared in **The Legacy** in October 1999 issue and is reprinted with permission.*

Indespensible Interstates – Part I.

With homage to an old song, I was cruising along in my automobile with some particular places to go. The traffic slowed down and soon I was creeping along like rush hour had come to mid day. The signs up ahead said the I-75 11 Mile bridge and exit ramps from the roadway to 11 Mile were closed. I was required to take a detour that made me late for my second appointment of the day. Like so many others, I had taken a favorite route for granted and cut things too close. Although I felt a little inconvenienced, my experiences couldn't compare to those of early drivers.

Dave Hunter, in his popular travel guide *Along I-75*, describes what it was like before such roads existed. "Prior to the construction of the Interstates, traveling long distances was painful, a trip from Detroit to Florida could easily take five to six days. Primary roads did not always go in straight lines – they often meandered around the countryside. Frequently, they were single lane and at every community along the way, traffic lights, stop signs and local cross traffic slowed the journey."

The Interstate Highway System was conceived in the late 30's during the Roosevelt Administration. Funding legislation enacted on June 29, 1956, allowed construction to begin on the "National System of Interstate and Defense Highways".

In spite of their advantages, Interstates were opposed by some people. Planners were required to do detailed studies to collect past and current data so they could make future forecasts. Major considerations included where people live, where they want to go, how they get there, where goods are produced, what markets the goods are sent to and how goods reach their final users.

Public hearings gave citizens a chance to provide input in road development. With their needs in mind, practical issues were addressed. For example, road numbers were carefully selected so even numbers are used for East – West routes and odd numbers for North – South routes.

While many people head South on I-75, others head North and enjoy more of our great state. Another acclaimed travel writer, Doris Scharfenberg, recalls taking many trips on the Interstate all the way up through our Upper Peninsula. *The Country Roads of Michigan* author said when we look at a map, the road that helps us zip along looks like a zipper running through our state.

"Our American psyche wants to zip along and we often think about how far we can get in a weekend," observed Scharfenberg. "Those of us who were not around before I-75 can only imagine the tremendous difference," she added.

We were both amazed at how many arenas, businesses, hotel/motels, outdoor theaters, tourist attractions and resorts have been built and achieved success due to the evolution of I-75. Scharfenberg pointed out that by taking short drives after exiting off the road, many other popular Michigan sites can be found nearby.

The part of I-75 that I was traveling on when the detour was required is also known as the Chrysler freeway. It was named after Walter Percy Chrysler, a founder and the first president of Chrysler Corporation. During his presidency, the Chrysler building was built in New York City and earned distinction as one of the country's largest buildings.

Keep cruising along, but don't forget to return to *The Legacy* for more insights about I-75, from a roads scholar and transportation expert.

*This article first appeared in **The Legacy** in May 2000 issue as part of "Michigan Roads" series and is reprinted with permission.*

Black Jesus Bears the Cross

"Color of the Cross will moisten our eyes and open our eyes making a huge difference in our lives."

~~Rev. Cecil L. "Chip" Murray
First African Methodist Episcopal
Church, Los Angeles pastor and
film producer

The *Color of the Cross* interjects race while telling the story of Jesus Christ's last 48 hours until his capture at Mount Gethsemane. It also focuses on the dynamics of family relationships rather than violence. By doing this, it makes a familiar story seem distinctly different.

"Do you think they're doing this because he is black?" That question, asked by Mary, Mother of Jesus (Debbi Morgan of *All My Children*, *Coach Carter* and *Woman Thou Art Loosed*), encourages the audience to think about related issues. Was the persecution of the son of God racially motivated or just due to his radical interpretations of the Torah? Is this film's alternative presentation of Jesus and his family more realistic than the traditional one?

"Our movie is not about dividing Christians but broadening their perspective," said Jean-Claude LaMarre, the Haitian-American director/writer/actor who wrote the screenplay and portrayed Jesus along with directing the film. "For centuries, Leonardo da Vinci's portrayal of Jesus [as a white man] has been widely accepted. We are offering an alternative image. There's room for all."

In the film, a black Jesus is portrayed as the wise leader. Others call him "master" and "rabbi" while he teaches important lessons and observes Jewish customs. As LaMarre acknowledged, seeing these depictions on screen "really blurs the lines that divide blacks and Jews in this country. We are part of the same history".

Although some people may view this film's portrayal of Jesus as being controversial, it is exciting to see a strong black leading man assume this positive role. The movie addresses four areas: Jesus and his disciples, the state of mind of the Romans occupying Judea, the issues facing the Rabbis in the Sanhedrin, and the family life of Joseph, Mary and their remaining children as they were affected by Jesus' persecution.

The film's attention to detail reflects a commitment to remain true to biblical and historical facts. Some historical data points to the fact that, based on the region where and times when Jesus lived, he might have been a black man.

All of the *Color of the Cross* principle cast members give first-rate performances. It is impossible to hear Morgan's piercing cries and not feel a mother's pain about the unjust treatment of her son. The cast also includes Ananda Lewis (MTVs *Total Request Live* and former talk show host) as Leah.

In spite of Hollywood connections made while working both in front of and behind the camera, LaMarre had to self-finance *Color of the Cross* in order to bring it to the screen. Although the film did not have a major Hollywood budget, it does have impressive cinematography featuring scenes shot outside of Los Angeles in areas resembling ancient Judea.

LaMarre, whose acting credits include *Malcolm X*, hopes *Color of the Cross* will be an empowering movie for youth like his son. He wonders whether it is too late for adults who spent decades viewing Jesus in a certain way to envision alternatives. Those willing to view *Color of the Cross* with an open mind will find it to be an entertaining experience suitable for the entire family. Plans are already underway for a sequel telling the resurrection story.

(Sidebar)
Color of the Cross tells a story that is familiar to most. "This movie is not about dividing people, it is about broadening their perspective," said the accomplished Haitian-American director/writer/actor who wrote the screenplay, directed the movie and also stars as Jesus in the film. "I believe Jesus was black. Through other people's eyes he may be white, Latino or Asian. We want to convey that it is not what the messenger looks like it is the message itself."

Color of the Cross
Release Date:
 October 27, 2006
Rated: PG 13
Highly Recommended
(For more information on "Color of the Cross" visit: www.colorofthecross.com)

This review article first appeared in ***about...time magazine*** *Vol. XXXIV (2006) No. 4 and is reprinted with permission.*

*RE*MARKABLE *RE*PRINTS

CHAPTER SIX

ENLIGHTENING
INSIGHTS

The World According to Alaina Jackson

Imagine growing up where blue and gold were primary colors. Wherever your studies or work led you to go, special ladies offered support and inspiration. That was not a fantasy but rather the reality of Soror Alaina Jackson.

"Since I was born, I saw the impact of sisterhood, scholarship and service," Jackson recalled. "I wanted to give back to the group that was such a crucial element to all the important parts of my life."

Jackson was proud to be part of a legacy of Sigma Gamma Rho sorors including her mother Frances C. Jackson, R.N., and grandmother Jessie Hubbard. "I saw what sisterhood meant to them and learned how to love it myself," said Jackson. Growing up with a lawyer father (Frank W. Jackson III., an attorney in labor law relations for Blue Cross Blue Shield of Michigan) and a college professor mother (an associate professor with Oakland University's School of Nursing), I was always inquisitive, but they encouraged me to discover things all by myself," she explained.

Being part of the Rho Sigma Rhoer Club also provided an opportunity for Jackson to interact with other positive role models, including Rho Sigma sorors Lillian Richardson and Ruby Coates Price. "Soror Richardson taught Rhoers about going to the source to obtain information," Jackson said. Richardson's entrepreneurial success inspired Jackson's pursuit of non-traditional career goals.

Jackson has already shown an ability to succeed. Her studies included learning opportunities with Northwestern University and Inca-Colegia in Peru, South America. After earning dual degrees in organizational communications and urban studies plus a minor in business, Jackson went to work for Robert Bosch. The Bosch Group employed more than 220,000 employees in more than 50 countries. It earned a reputation for "forward thinking technology" and "trail-blazing inventions" including ignition plugs and fire alarm systems.

As a management trainee, Jackson rotated to different departments and gained valuable insights. She started off in Grand Rapids where sorors in the western Michigan region bonded together although a graduate chapter did not exist.

It was part of her employer's requirements for Jackson to spend time working abroad. She went to Germany with basic knowledge about the country and its culture. Jackson was, however, fluent in three languages — English, German and Spanish.

The time spent in a different country exceeded her expectations. "I was surprised about the level of diversity reflected in political thought as well as on social economic levels," Jackson recalled. The society's structure meant company presidents and janitors were entitled to the same level of health insurance. Higher education was available to everyone in spite of income level.

Lonely Planet's Guide to Germany says balancing "cultural improvement and modernization with upholding cultural traditions" is the German way. It is a "traditionally meat-and-potatoes kind of country" where "beer is a national beverage and cultural phenomenon". The guide added that united "Germany is working toward true unity in typically sedulous fashion".

While working in Stuttgart as a Bosch Project Manager from August 2002 – April 2003, living in its Ditzingen suburb, Jackson saw the dynamics of German politics. "It was virtually unheard of not to be part of the political process so everyone took an interest in the candidates running for national election," Jackson said. Her language fluency helped when following news stories reflecting candidates' efforts to distinguish themselves by stating their platforms. The result of their efforts was an informed voting public.

One of Jackson's biggest discoveries was that "the same spirit of sisterhood" existed in Germany. She experienced "a very strong Sigma presence" in Chicago as an undergrad prospect and then upon joining the sorority in June 2000. Leadership skills were developed while serving as tamiochus and anti-basileus. In Grand Rapids, as a member-at-large, Jackson learned about long-distance Sigma love. Related reflections gave experiences with sorors in Germany added significance.

"We really have something special. The more I have traveled, the more I have appreciated this," Jackson acknowledged. "I had an overwhelming sense of pride and joy to know that not only were my sorors there, they were living up to the standards of our founders," she added.

Jackson was also impressed with the creativity sorors in Germany showed related to community service projects. Not having lots of homeless people meant there were not shelters everywhere in need of assistance. "The level of need was not the same as we have experienced in the United States because the government takes care of more related things," Jackson observed. She said a lot of the sorors abroad were in the military. Others had family members who were officers. Some community service projects included baking cookies for local children and encouraging people to unite in prayer in response to the war in Iraq.

Although Jackson was a stranger to Germany, she was not treated like one. Sorors welcomed her into their homes and checked in periodically. Her demanding job involved training experts to be better managers. Jackson managed all of the challenges while being thankful to have sisters nearby.

Back in the U.S.A., Jackson settled in as a Bosch financial analyst headquartered in the Farmington Hills suburb of Detroit. She and her team assisted with business planning for Indiana, Massachusetts and Mexico plants. Since returning home, Jackson studied Japanese in preparation for other international opportunities.

After contemplating working abroad again, Jackson expressed the desire to return to Germany to visit. "Everyone should take at least six weeks to see Europe in depth," said the experienced traveler. Jackson enjoyed spending time in Germany's vibrant capital city of Berlin and Paris, France. She also enjoyed studying in Frankfurt and Bonn. "People traveled from county to country over there the way we do from state to state over here," Jackson reported.

At press time, Jackson eagerly anticipated another international adventure. She was confirming plans for spending months working in Juarez, Mexico. "I am excited because it will be close to Central America but just south of El Paso, Texas," Jackson acknowledged. "I enjoy speaking Spanish and the Hispanic culture," she said. "I am hoping to be able to continue the tradition of meeting Sigma sorors wherever I go."

"I hope that telling my story will remind others they should look for their sorors when they travel or move," said Jackson. Remember that, wherever Sigma Gamma Rho sorors go, there are opportunities to experience how bonds of sisterhood transcend geographic boundaries plus language/cultural differences throughout the world.

*This article first appeared in **The Aurora** magazine (the official international publication of Sigma Gamma Rho Sorority, Inc.) in the Spring/Summer 2004 issue as part of the "Golden Glimpses Across the Globe" cover story series and is reprinted with permission.*

Idlewild Memories

In my junior high and teen years, getting away to the country became synonymous with Idlewild trips. My family and friends would pack up the car and travel to the rural Northwestern Michigan town in Lake County. When approaching this special area, we looked forward to adventure-filled days and peaceful nights.

I remember putting on a bright orange life jacket and joining my Uncle Raymond on his boat. Being a skilled fisherman, he expertly caught the catch of the day. I spent quality time with a favorite relative admiring the beauty of the great outdoors and sometimes pitying the ones that didn't get away.

Once on a bike ride, the way I rode briefly made me a legend in those parts. Some tourists, in awe of the view, nearly ran into me with their car. This collision was avoided when I took an unexpected detour without missing a beat. I fearlessly pedaled down near the water's edge before returning to the road. My cousins expressed admiration for the bike riding abilities no one, including me, knew that I had.

When I needed to forget about work demands and complete my Masters' degree project, like Henry David Thoreau who discovered Walden Pond, my solitude was sought in the woods. Idlewild provided a welcome change of pace where interruptions could be avoided and nature walks refreshed a weary soul. To my delight, I realized a higher level of productivity in that special place.

Back in the day, Idlewild was more than a place for this city girl to seek country pleasures or make a great escape. In the 1950s and 1960s, this site near Highway 10 was a hot spot for entertainment started in an earlier decade.

You can return to that time by taking a trip to nearby Henry Ford Greenfield Village and the "Idlewild Clubhouse" this summer. That attraction showcases dramatic performances, poetry readings, art exhibits and music to evoke the atmosphere of the 1920's. Through August 20, you can be transported on the "Idlewild Excursion Coach" from the entrance to the Clubhouse celebrating another era.

Visitors will be treated to lively interactions with well-known personalities of the day such as W.E.B. DuBois and will be presented with the artistic works of the likes of Langston Hughes, Louis Armstrong and Zora Neale Hurston. "Idlewilders" will walk through Greenfield Village and encourage families to drop by the Clubhouse.

DuBois and other famous African-Americans, including celebrities and entertainers, purchased land in Idlewild at a time when segregation laws made it impossible for them to enjoy vacationing elsewhere. In the same picturesque area that inspired my Mother and her younger brother to purchase cottages, men and women of the Harlem Renaissance bought property. They traveled from Detroit, Chicago and beyond to relax in a place where they were also respected.

"The Harlem Renaissance was a significant movement influencing not only African-American culture but America's culture; its influences are still being felt today," said Oliver Ragsdale, Jr., President of The Arts League of Michigan. The Clubhouse is a collaboration between the League and Henry Ford Museum & Greenfield Village. It is part of the Harlem Renaissance program made possible by a grant from the Community Foundation for Southeastern Michigan. For more information about the project and to receive group discount coupons, call The Arts League of Michigan at (313) 964-1670.

*This article first appeared in **The Legacy** in August 2000 issue as part of "Highlights and Insights" and is reprinted with permission.*

Legends in the Game
Reflections of Black Professional
Basketball Champions

"The unique style of play exhibited by African-American basketball players beginning in the 1920s greatly impacted the game played by NBA athletes today...These talented men and women helped break down the color barrier and made it possible for a new generation of athletes to experience even greater success in the NBA and WNBA. They not only changed the game, but they also changed the fabric of American life."

~~ U.S. Rep. Carolyn Cheeks Kilpatrick (MI)

A family friend often said, "The camera takes what it sees and the mirror shows what's really there". When you look in the mirror, what do you see?

I talked with three black professional basketball legends able to still see colorful memories of the past and realistic perspectives of the present while envisioning a brighter future. After all of these years, the terrific trio – namely John Isaacs, Frank Washington and Dr. John L. Kline – still got game and the world needs to know it.

Resolutions Salute Unsung Heroes and Heroines

Many people are unaware that this year will mark the first anniversary of the passage of two distinctive joint congressional resolutions – H. CON RES 59 (passed on October 6, 2005 by voice vote) and SEN. RES 57 (passed on December 22, 2005 by unanimous consent). Both of them provided some long overdue recognition for the contributions of Black professional basketball players.

U.S. Congresswoman Carolyn Cheeks Kilpatrick (MI), house bill sponsor, wrote the following explanation of significance in a letter to National Basketball Association (NBA) Commissioner David Stern. "The resolution acknowledges the unique style of play exhibited by African American basketball players beginning in the 1920's that greatly impacted the game played by NBA athletes today...These talented men and women helped break down the color barrier and made it possible for a new generation of athletes to experience an even greater success in the NBA and WNBA. They not only changed the game, but they also changed the fabric of American life." The letter was sent in fulfillment of a resolution statement indicating the NBA and Naismith Memorial Basketball Hall of Fame should receive copies of the historic document.

The resolutions also cited the individual accomplishments of African American basketball legends including Tarzan Cooper, Pop Gates, Isaacs, Marques Haynes and Goose Tatum. Teams cited included the New York Rens, Harlem Clowns and Harlem Globetrotters plus women's teams such as the Chicago Romas.

In addition, the resolution saluted efforts of Kline and his Black Legends of Professional Basketball Foundation (BLPBF) for work related to honoring Black professional basketball pioneers and encouraging others to add them to their hall of fame rosters. For instance, it was publicly acknowledged that Kline and his foundation played an instrumental effort by leading a grassroots campaign supporting Haynes' Naismith Memorial Basketball Hall of Fame induction. That induction opened the door for future ones for the Harlem Globetrotters and Lynette Woodard, the first female Harlem Globetrotter.

There will be several resolution anniversary-linked celebrations in 2007. Kline plans to publish *Black Pawns in the Cold War*, a non fiction book that takes a critical look at U.S. States Department strategy and its practices related to African-American athletes and entertainers. A traveling exhibition featuring artifacts and photographs will be developed for shows at venues throughout the country. A documentary was being filmed about the Black basketball legends' experiences. Interviews were being conducted for a publication featuring reflections, present activities and future objectives.

Event planning was underway for August 18, 2007 gala uniting Black professional basketball legends with current NBA/WNBA players and supporters. At press time, Kline was talking with potential sponsors for the planned celebration components but welcomed hearing from others. For additional information, call the BLPBF headquarters at 313.822.8208. In the meantime, read on to learn more about the resolutions and terrific trio who excelled both on and off the court in ways impacting the lives of many others.

Black Basketball Resolutions Highlights

According to GovTrack, the House and Senate must both pass concurrent resolutions. They don't require the president's signature or have the force of law. They do, however, provide a means to express a sentiment of Congress/impact internal rules. H. CON. RES 59 was introduced by Kilpatrick and supported by at least 50 other legislators including U.S. Congressmen John Conyers, Jr. (MI) and Charles Rangel (NY). S. CON RES 57 was introduced by U.S. Senator Debbie Stabenow (MI) and supported by her esteemed colleague, Carl Levin (MI). This was noteworthy on several counts because, as GovTrack explained, countless senate bills were referred to committee before presentation to the entire body but never made it out of committee.

Kline's tenacity, along with his supporters, played an instrumental role in the resolution passage. A grassroots campaign resulted in letters of support being obtained from community leaders and citizens throughout the country. Exhibits and public presentations at libraries, institutions of learning and other community centers also enhanced awareness of the grassroots campaign.

The successful passage of resolutions that many people believed would never make it out of committee should serve as a source of inspiration. It is proof positive that the hard work of dedicated citizens can earn recognition for deserving organizations and individuals from our leaders in Washington D.C.

The "Boy Wonder" Really Outstanding Man

John Isaacs had a nickname that indicated he was capable of fantastic feats on the basketball court. Teams who delighted in seeing the "Boy Wonder" exhibiting his skills as a passer really had something to cheer about. He moved from being just another player chosen by Bob Douglas to star status as a member of the New York Rens World Professional Basketball Tournament winning team in 1939. The all-black Rens resoundingly defeated the all-white Osh Kosh All Stars.

Although "boy" was part of his nickname, Isaacs didn't see one when he looked in the mirror. Consequentially, he took exception to being called "boy" by racists encountered on the road. Isaacs acknowledged thinking quick on his feet and having a good sense of humor were essential survival skills. Yet, at times, the Panama native expressed himself in ways reflecting the "New York [spirit] rising up" in him. After all Isaacs had lived in the U.S. since he was 5.

On one occasion, Isaacs talked back to a ticket agent who insisted he reenter a train station through the "Colored's entrance" in order to obtain a train ticket to Atlanta. Friends pointed out to him later that such freedom of expression could have had dire consequences. But Isaacs still doesn't regret sharing his views about the need for times to change.

"Overall it was a rewarding and learning process being on the road," said the man many now affectionately call "Mr. I". In addition to encountering negative experiences below the "cotton curtain" or Mason Dixon line in southern states, Isaacs was able to establish positive relationships with people he still hears from decades later. During our interview, he shared greetings received for his 91st birthday celebration on September 30, 2006.

Isaacs appeared to be more excited about being honored by Empowerment

Through Recognition for achievements including working with the Madison Square Boys and Girls Club in the Bronx for more than 40 years. The center named their gym the "John 'Boy Wonder' Isaacs Gymnasium" in honor of his contributions.

In addition to counseling youth, Isaacs cohosts a radio program where he shares pearls of wisdom. "Basketball is a fun game," Isaacs observed. "It's about using your brain against your opponent and you do have to play defense."

Much More Than Another Pop Sensation

"As a young man playing with some of the greatest basketball players in the world, they taught me a lot," acknowledged Frank Washington. He played professional basketball from approximately 1939 – 1960 with four years spent in the Navy and playing for the service team.

Washington's name appeared on professional basketball team rosters for the New York Rens, Washington Lickman Bears and Philadelphia Lumberjacks. He fondly remembers many things about playing for the Harlem Globetrotters.

"Anyone would enjoy traveling around the world four times when everything was first class and you met heads of state and leaders of the world," Washington stated. "We did things that would never have been done otherwise while making $300 or $400 a month."

In this basketball legend's mind, there was no comparison between the game when he played and now. "Players now get one hundred million before even putting on a pair of shoes," Washington stated. Harlem Globetrotter Owner Abe Saperstein didn't even pay his players as much as the entertainers who performed at half time. "I am kind of happy to see owner's feet held to the fire now," Washington admitted.

Back in the day, being on the road was a grueling experience. "People today have no idea how we suffered in the years basketball was getting started," Washington said. "We rode on a bus across country all year in all kinds of weather with no heat or air conditioning."

The Philadelphia native recalls confrontations with racism both at home and abroad. The team couldn't get a hotel room in his hometown because folks taking reservations hadn't realized Harlem Globetrotters were Black. When riding through Idaho, a deli clerk allowed Washington to purchase bologna for sandwiches but claimed milk in plain sight wasn't for "colored folks".

"In the 1950's, I was treated so well many places [outside the United States], I wouldn't have known I was Black without looking in the mirror if it hadn't been for racism experienced in America and England," Washington revealed.

Just as Washington kept on striving while playing professional basketball, he achieved success off the court while working for a major soft drink manufacturer. His humanitarian spirit led to sponsoring golf tournaments for youth.

"It's a shame that basketball has forgotten about us," said a man willing to share his memories and much more. "If it hadn't been for us, there would be no NBA as we know it."

Determined to Keep Jumpin' Ahead

"We enjoyed playing so much that some of us might have paid the owner to keep on doing it," said the hall of famer and former

Harlem Globetrotter also known as Jumpin'
Johnny Kline.

Kline recalls that the team had an
entertaining way of dealing with hecklers who
frequently used the N-word or made other
derogatory remarks. "We would start a game
of baseball in front of him and intentionally
make the catcher miss the ball," he explained.
"It would splash into his drink or cause the
guy to waste food."

The team efforts confirmed Kline's
claim that professional basketball was a team
sport when he played in 1953 – 59. "The
individual competition for dollars and star
status takes the team aspect out of things so
players now are pressed to be taller, faster and
stronger." Another noteworthy distinction
between then and now is players used to stay
together on teams for 8 or 9 years and build a
rapport.

Kline spent time bonding with team-
mates while experiencing many cultures
throughout the world. As a young man, he
didn't always realize the significance of events
evolving around him. Decades later, when
others talked about historic occurrences,
Kline remembered being in the midst of
them. While in the Philippines, Kline read
signs saying "Yankee Go Home" without

their full meaning sinking in. He immediately understood, however, the warm sentiments of approximately 300 Australian aborigines who hosted a party in his team's honor.

"The facts of history that we can share with current players are history that is relevant to all of us," said Kline. Most of all, he hopes passage of the resolutions will afford an opportunity to spend quality time enhancing awareness.

In the meantime, Kline has continued to make plans for projects benefiting his native Detroit community and country. "There were programs launched through the Black Legends of Professional Basketball Foundation, including our Youth Athletic Enrichment Program, that experts said could serve as national models," Kline pointed out. "We have already effectively worked with thousands of boys and girls and with more funding a lot more could be reached." BLPBF also honored many barnstorming and NBA players with induction into its hall of fame.

"It is not just about me," Kline concluded. "Many others loved the sport and devoted their lives to it…I want our young and future generations to be aware of their legacy."

*This article first appeared in **about...time** magazine Vol. XXXV (2007) No. 1 and is reprinted with permission.*

Williamsburg Adventure Transcends Time

While America celebrated Independence Day 2003, a trip for an innovative H-H Family Reunion led to new discoveries of revolutionary history.

My destination was Williamsburg, Virginia. It was located in "The Historic Triangle" which included Jamestown and Yorktown. This popular tourist area allowed visitors to enjoy amenities of modern resorts and favorite restaurants near acclaimed amusements parks before heading down the road to world-renowned historic sites.

My favorite tourist attraction was Colonial Williamsburg. It claimed to be America's largest living history museum and offered the opportunity to experience life in the 18th century.

From 1699 to 1780, Williamsburg was the capital of Great Britain's largest and most prosperous colony. Colonial Williamsburg allowed guests to journey back to a significant turning point in our history.

Although my first trip to Colonial Williamsburg lasted only one day and a half, it was time well spent. The amazing site consisted of 301-acres with hundreds of original or recreated buildings, gardens and public greens. "People of the past" and other costumed residents strolled through the area while interacting with guests. These special people included political leaders such as Thomas Jefferson and Patrick Henry plus enslaved children and adults. Guests didn't just hear about the news they became part of it by participating in activities such as the "Order in the Court" mock trial reenactment. Hands-on-opportunities included making crafts or helping tradesman do their jobs. Evening entertainment featured Colonial Performances such as "Papa Said, Mama Said" with 18th century free and enslaved Black people reflecting on lessons taught by their elders. After a Fourth of July concert, featuring The Colonial Williamsburg Fifes and Drums, the sky lit up with a fireworks display in Market Square.

"I have seen a lot of history but there are still many things I haven't seen," acknowledged H-H Washington D.C./Maryland/Virginia Chapter President Lawrence Branch.

Although Branch and other chapter members regularly visited the area, none of them lived in the immediate vicinity. "This was our first attempt at a destination family reunion and it required adjusting our expectations to suit remote challenges," he explained.

"It is important to find a location with standards to make everyone happy then maintain effective communication and coordination with people at the site," Branch added.

My cousin also shared insights reflecting the critical need for being able to quickly implement destination family reunion back up plans.

The host group had originally scheduled activities at Carter's Grove. After invitations had already been extended, they had to change those plans.

The popular site, located approximately 8 miles southeast of Williamsburg, closed for renovations.

Although everyone regretted canceling the Carter's Grove mansion and slave quarters visit, they made other plans to share history and African-American legacies. These plans included having family banquet entertainment center around an interactive storytelling and African instrument performance. My Williamsburg adventure allowed me to enjoy a family tradition with a new twist. Next year the H-H Family Reunion returns to Detroit where it originated in 1980 and featured a Belle Isle picnic. Future plans for this history buff include scheduling another visit to the area for our first destination family reunion.

For additional information about Williamsburg, call (800) 368-6511 or visit www.VisitWilliamsburg.com. To prepare for a Colonial Williamsburg journey, call 800-HISTORY or visit www.colonial-williamsburg.org.

*This article first appeared in **The Michigan FrontPage** in August 15, 2003 issue and is reprinted with permission.*

*RE*MARKABLE
*RE*PRINTS

CHAPTER SEVEN

YOUTH
SUPPORTERS

Smiling Faces Enjoy Healthy Reading: Children's Book Author Odessa M. Groves, Ed.D. Presents Health Facts Along With Humorous Insights

"I have never seen anything like it," said Elizabeth Stone, owner of Elizabeth Stone Gallery for the Fine Art of Children's Book Illustration. 'This book reflects a special niche and needs to be promoted through dedicated dentists' offices."

Stone praised the critically acclaimed *Toothbrush, Toothpaste and Floss* children's book by Soror Odessa M. Groves, Ed.D. that was featured during an author's event at her gallery. It shared dental hygiene facts in an ingenious way for elementary school children. Toothbrush narrated the story about spending time with Toothpaste and Floss while they "play in the mouth". Enlightening illustrations showed the proper techniques for handling dental hygiene.

"Dr. Dentist told us to keep doing our job everyday," reported Toothpaste. "We all felt very important knowing that we help to keep the teeth clean."

Toothbrush has also earned rave reviews from book reviewers and members of its target audience. "I love to read because it helps me learn about a lot of things," said nine-year-old Tyler Dominique Eanes. "This book was nice and funny with drawings that looked just like my teeth and other people's teeth." The third grade honor roll student at the Clara W. Rutherford Academy enjoys writing her own stories and drawing characters for them. "I like surprises and I enjoyed reading it to my little sister who is five." The surprise recipient of a Bill Clinton Presidential Award, presented in her school auditorium, looks forward to reading other books by Groves. She said *Toothbrush* ranks right up there with her all-time favorite book, *The Cat in the Hat.*

Groves is especially interested in working with children like Eanes who are of elementary through intermediate grade age levels. A career as an educator with the Detroit Public Schools System opened her eyes to post-retirement teaching alternatives. She has encouraged Eanes and other youths to participate in Rho Sigma Chapter's literacy events at community centers and bookstores. The main focus now is to deliver information to assist children during their different stages of growth and development. "I am always teaching lessons," Groves explained. "By using humor with a message, learning doesn't have to be dry and boring."

A double major in art gives Groves the ability to illustrate her own books. She says life as a published author has exceeded expectations and helped her to reach another creative plateau. "I plan to continue writing books in different styles to reach my young audiences," said Groves, who diligently researches her books and interviews professionals to verify data. "What I enjoy most is taking a crazy subject and seeing where I can go with it." An entertaining example is her ***Ketchup and French Fry*** book highlighting the backgrounds of these children's favorites and nutrition insights.

During October 2002, National Dental Hygiene Month, Groves made public appearances throughout the Metropolitan Detroit area. "I am growing and learning myself while having fun sharing with others," she acknowledged.

The American Dental Association (ADA)'s designation of February as National Children's Dental Health Month (NCDHM) is avidly supported by Groves. "We need to start making children aware that having good dental hygiene habits can help them be healthier adults," said Groves.

The annual observance promoting children's dental health awareness began as a one-day event in Cleveland, Ohio on Feb. 3, 1941. During that same year, Children's Dental Health Week was designated as Feb. 3 – 7 in Akron, Ohio.

The American Dental Association held the first national observance of Children's Dental Health Day on Feb. 8, 1949. The single day observance became a week-long event in 1955. In 1981, the program was extended to a month-long celebration known today as NCDHM.

The NCDHM 2003 theme is "Don't Let Your Smile Become Extinct". NCDHM messages reach millions of people in com-munities across the country and armed services bases abroad. Local observances include poster/coloring/essay contests, health fairs, free dental screenings, museum exhibits, classroom presentations and dental office tours.

The ADA produces program planning kits and shares NCDHM celebration materials through its web site at ada.org. Check out the ADA Kids' Corner and meet Dudley the

Dragon. Dudley's top three tips, shared through fun activities, are listed below.

- ✓ Brush and floss each day.
- ✓ Eat nutritious foods.
- ✓ Have regular dental checkups.

At press time, Groves was working on creating more unique children's books. Notable among them is another dental-health-related adventure. She is trying new things with illustrating characters and experimenting with the use of color. Toothbrush and her other creations will be featured during winter appearances at metropolitan Detroit area bookstores, cultural centers and libraries.

*This article first appeared in **The AURORA** magazine in Winter/Spring 2003 issue and is reprinted with permission.*

Dittrich Plus KISS Equals
Financial Success

When Harold (Hal) G. Dittrich was about 8 or 9 years old, his dad made an offer a wise son couldn't refuse: "If you save some money, I'll match it". Dittrich ended up having a small amount to invest in the stock market.

Focusing on investing at an early age became a family tradition carried on with his sons, Jason and Shawn. They grew up knowledgeable about financial matters and prepared to assist with operating the family business, Dittrich Furs, with locations in Detroit and Bloomfield Hills.

Dittrich Furs has subsequently helped kids make sense out of saving dollars. Last year, CEO Hal Dittrich worked with Ron Banks of the Dramatics who introduced him to his brother, Mike, and they founded Kids Investing in Simple Solutions (KISS).

"Children are not taught about financial matters in schools and may not have adults they can turn to for guidance," said Dittrich. "I thought it would be good for everyone to learn basics about how to put some money away."

KISS grew out of a goal to share financial insights with the Dittrich extended family of employees, customers and the metropolitan Detroit community. Classes included approximately 18 kids from 9-16 years of age. Guest speakers were financial service professionals who made presentations about creating, managing and investing money.

The National Endowment for the Education Foundation showed support for students involved in KISS. Two students applied for scholarships. An award was given for the best investor. Last summer, there were seven instructors for classes at five sites including schools and a recreation center. In 2004, growth will be continued with expansion to 10 sites.

"Dittrich is our main sponsor," said KISS Program Director/Coordinator Mike Banks. "We are very lucky to have such a supportive man committed to the program."

Additional funds are needed to reach a more diverse audience and expand into churches. "We would welcome hearing from private or individual sponsors," said Banks. For more information about KISS, call 313-478-4955.

Emil Dittrich, a furrier from London, opened the doors of Dittrich Furs in 1893. Now located on Third Avenue in the fifth generation of family leadership, it is the oldest family-owned retail business in Detroit. Dittrich Furs has grown to house one of the country's largest fur collections. It has consistently provided a full range of services including the design and manufacturing of fur garments, repairing and restyling of older garments and state-of-the-art cleaning and storage. Although Dittrich Furs has changed dramatically since 1893, the family atmosphere and dedication to quality and craftsmanship remain the same.

"It makes you feel good to help kids," said Dittrich whose business also sponsored two local baseball teams. In addition there have been other charitable efforts including supporting BUOY 13 (Business United with Officers for Youths), Jack's Place for Kids' autistic children programs and Children's Hospital's "Christmas is for Kids".

Dittrich's community service record reflects a commitment to supporting people of all ages. Furs are regularly donated for charity and church fundraisers. As a member of the New Center Council, Dittrich sponsored an annual flower bed on West Grand

Boulevard. It also hosted a Breast Cancer Awareness program when a crowd gathered in the store for an informative session, with donations going to the Karmanos Center. "The majority of our employees have lived in Detroit and enjoyed being a part of this community," Dittrich said.

The Fur History in Detroit found on www.dittrichfurs.com offers more insights about the area's past and serves as a resource for students. Dittrich plans to remain committed to encouraging others to invest in opportunities promoting financial success and future growth.

*This article first appeared in **Michigan Chronicle** and **The Michigan FrontPage** "A Heart for the Holidays" insert in December 17-23, 2003 issue and is reprinted with permission.*

Visionary Villagers Celebrate 25th Anniversary

While envisioning the future, Alkebu-Lan Village is taking time out to celebrate its past. The four-day celebration kicks off with Illumination, an African-centered black-tie affair in the village at 7701 Harper on June 5. Illumination features a 5 p.m. reception, 6 p.m. dinner/program and 9 – 11 p.m. after-glow. Michigan State University African and African American Studies Professor Jualynne E. Dobson is the keynote speaker. Tickets are $125 per person.

Call 313-921-1616 for additional information about Illumination and other celebration events. They include a June 6 open house, June 7 Motor City National Martial Arts Tournament and June 8 Showcase of the Academy of the Arts.

"It takes 25 years to establish yourself," said Marvis Cofield, CEO, Alkebu-Lan Village. "We now have the history, experience and data so we can collate that information to keep moving in the right direction...if you don't know you can't grow."

Alkebu-Lan Village has grown from its humble beginnings in 1978 as a martial arts federation to a village with the holistic approach for services to children and their families. Martial arts focuses on structured physical activity linked to self-control. Villagers also learn lessons that impact their mind and spirit.

"In most cases, young folks don't want to go home because it is definitely their village," acknowledged Cofield. "We offer them a forum to express themselves and listen to their needs when designing programs."

The programs include African dance and drumming classes, drama, music, tutorial services and home economics/life skills classes.

Alkebu-Lan Village is truly a community center for east-side residents. The large, still evolving, facility features a skating rink, cafeteria and many meeting rooms. It is open year-round and seeks to enhance education received in the classroom.

During the celebration on Friday, Alkebu-Lan Village opens the doors for its Entrepreneurship Mini Mall. Young people will have a place to set up shop and run their business.

"Imagine how a 14-year-old will feel when he can pass out his business cards and invite customers to visit him at work," Cofield said. "We need to train boys and girls to think like business people and help them to become successful so they can teach others."

Cofield knows first-hand about being an enterprising young man. His community service began at age 14. He was supported by his parents and inspired by "heroes", Inner City Sub-Center founders Paul Taylor and David Booker. The center, still striving today, helped enhance self-esteem and reinforce survival basics.

"Our ancestors were wise and they gave us astrology, astronomy, the arts and so much more," said former Detroit Public Schools board member Cofield. "Once you find out you were the first, not the last, that makes you feel good. We go back over a million years and need to embrace our rich cultural heritage and ties to motherland Africa."

Cofield looks forward to continuing to lead a dedicated team of eight full-time employees, 20 part-timers and a host of volunteers.

Anyone interested in supporting the team should call 313-921-1616.

*This article first appeared in **The Michigan FrontPage** in June 6, 2003 issue and is reprinted with permission.*

Collector Shares Treasures
With Community

During this holiday season when many wonder what they will receive, let's salute someone who shares with others. While Allean H. House welcomed two biological children and 22 foster children into her home over a 40-year span, people often inquired about why collectibles were within their reach.

"I wanted my children to experience things they could benefit from knowing about later in life," she responded.

The retired Inkster Public Schools educator shared collectibles throughout Metropolitan Detroit. They included artifacts, books, dolls, photos, models, posters and scrapbooks featuring African-Americans and women. Hundreds of items, some of which she loaned out, were collected during extensive travels.

People strolling through Northland Shopping Center and Trapper's Alley have viewed special exhibits with complementary programs coordinated by House.

For decades, her February African-American History Month and March Women's History Month showcases appeared at a variety of venues. Some of them were

YWCA of Highland Park, Henry Ford Centennial Library in Dearborn plus Considine Recreation Center, Hartford Memorial Baptist Church and Lewis College of Business in Detroit. House frequently worked with organizations creating special ways to link sharing history with goals. She has won awards and special recognition for her efforts.

In January 2003, House revived the Sigma Gamma Rho Sorority, Inc. (Rho Sigma Chapter) Carver Day Celebration. It was held at the Austin W. Curtis Museum, the site honoring Dr. George Washington Carver's only living protégé and his mentor.

"Dr. Curtis fondly remembers joining his friend when he spoke to students for her programs," revealed Mary Jones of the museum and House of Beauty Hair Mall where it is located now. "It is fitting she helped us open the doors for the museum's first public event."

In February, House complemented the African-American History Month exhibit she coordinated for DAZS Coalition of Black Greek Women at Considine with a program. "African-Americans Who Made A Difference" featured local professionals sharing success stories with youth.

DAZS President June Sutton also expressed her gratitude for House's efforts related to a Women's History Month exhibit coordinated with The Ellington-White Group and Northwest Activities Center.

House created Rho Sigma's "Color Carver's World" K-6 grades coloring contest. All contest participants will receive a recognition award. Independent judges will select winners for special prizes from entries displayed as part of a month-long January 2004 exhibit at Considine.

All award distribution is scheduled for Saturday, Jan. 10, during a noon interactive program. Everyone is encouraged to attend the free program with refreshments at Considine. For additional information, call 313-592-0262.

"If she commits to something, you can count on her to do it," said Rho Sigma Basileus (President) Claudia M. Clark. "She works diligently and will not stop until the work is done."

House is an active past basileus who serves on many committees and represents the chapter to several affiliate organizations including DAZS and DABO. She is also Rho Sigma Foundation treasurer and in her second term as National Pan-Hellenic Council of Metropolitan Detroit president.

"When I think of Mrs. House, I think of someone who has given her heart to family and community," said John Aaron, president of Alabama A & M Alumni Association's Detroit Renaissance Chapter. He also acknowledged that both House and her husband, who died in a car accident while traveling to their school's Founder's Day Celebration, were "strong supporters" of their undergraduate alma mater.

"She helped organize the Detroit Renaissance Chapter. If I was looking for a person to serve as a role model for my children or to highly recommend, it would be none other than Allean H. House," Aaron said.

Growing up watching my mother, it was easy to see sharing skills and treasures enhanced their value. Community service handled in a creative way was fun and rewarding. These valuable lessons were priceless treasures, too.

*This article first appeared in **The Michigan FrontPage** in December 26, 2003 issue and is reprinted with permission.*

*RE*MARKABLE
*RE*PRINTS

CHAPTER EIGHT

HOLIDAY
FOCUS

Seaberry Takes Stress Out of Holidays

Take a look at your calendar/ datebook for this month and what do you see? Probably lots of holiday activities during hectic weeks jam-packed with seeing friends and family. All of that excitement can lead to stress. Judy Seaberry, author of *Is Your Family dys Functional?*, has some tips that can help take the stress out of your holiday season.

Seaberry retired in 2003 and began to indulge her passion in writing. The mother of two sons has been divorced for almost 20 years. Seaberry believes her sense of humor has helped when dealing with "the storms of life". One of her favorite sayings is "Don't quit".

"Some time ago, a friend and I began to discuss dysfunctional families," Seaberry recalled. There was a spirited debate due to her friend's contention that all families were dysfunctional. Initially, Seaberry disagreed with her but later related thoughts reflected a change of opinion. "I acknowledged her point of view, and then we began to debate the level at which some families function, and from those discussions an idea was formed," Seaberry explained. "Not being a psychologist or a trained professional, these instances all came from my musings and vivid imagination."

Seaberry's book is in fact a hilarious treasury of comparisons and contrasts between function and dysfunction revealed through insights and illustrations. "First, I list the dysfunctional way to handle a situation then the functional way to relate; the two are wildly different and this was done with intention," she stated. "Of course, the lesson here, as with most situations, is balance."

It would be easy for Seaberry to just say that and continue on her merry way. Seaberry, however, took the time to share the following dys~holiday memories, stressful holiday realities and happy holiday celebration tips.

Dys~Holiday Memories

Dys~Holiday memory ~Child is getting the same present year after year.

Dys~Holiday memory ~Adolescent is wearing clothes to school that everyone else has worn there.
Dys~Holiday memory ~Adult fight breaks out after too much eggnog.

Stressful Holiday Realities

No money
Unresolved sibling rivalry
Unwarranted criticisms
An ex shows up to dinner with a brother/
  sister
Relatives packing up plates before everyone
  else has eaten
Unsolicited drunken advice on relationships
Late arrivals with uninvited guests

Happy Holiday Celebration Tips

Remember that the dysfunctional way is to do
  the opposite of all these things.
Make a list
Set budget
Shop early

Use discipline
Plan your holiday

For additional information about Seaberry or to order copies of her book visit www.judyseaberry.com or call 313.778.1550. Keep in mind her main goal for writing the book was to provide motivation for "a healing" to occur after experiencing "opportunity to look at someone else's house and realize my home wasn't so bad". Seaberry observed that it is important to reach out to others in order not to be lonely during the holiday season.

*This article first appeared in **Legacy News** in December 2007 issue and is reprinted with permission.*

National Poetry Observances
Extend To All Year

This year is an extra special one for poets and poetry lovers nationally and locally. The Academy of American Poets announced plans to launch a Web-based National Poetry Almanac that provides poetry highlights, activities, ideas and history for individual exploration/classroom use.

"The National Poetry Almanac will extend the celebration of poetry from April to all year round," observed the Academy's Executive Director Tree Swenson. It established April as National Poetry Month in 1996. The Almanac's launch was planned to tie in with the celebration. For additional information, visit www.poets.org/npm.

The Sixth Annual Young People's Poetry Week (April 12 – 18), sponsored by the Children's Book Council, is another national observance that highlights poetry's value to children and young adults. It encourages the public to bring more poetry into the home, classroom and childcare centers. The Poetry Week's official poet, Jane Yolen, can be contacted with questions during National Poetry Month. Contact www.cbcbooks.org or www.janeyolen.com for details.

Locally, InsideOut Literary Arts Project focuses on poetry throughout the year. "We believe in the words of the great Irish poet William Butler Yeats that education is not the filling of a pail but the lighting of a fire," explained InsideOut Executive Director/Founder Dr. Terry M. Blackhawk. "Our mission is to engage students with the pleasure and power of language and to celebrate their accomplishments in the community at large."

Since its founding in 1995, InsideOut has served approximately 2400 children annually through its distinctive non-profit writers-in-residence program. Talented poets and writers, representing diverse back-grounds, are dedicated to bringing creative experiences to children in their classrooms. "The real joy of working with kids is watching their faces when they learn they already have something to say others feel is significant," acknowledged InsideOut Hutchinson Elementary School Writer-in-Residence Aria Dammons. "One of the real assets of this program is when students see their words in print and it validates they can be creative," added the Hamtramck resident who worked with four schools over the years.

Another Hamtramck resident, Matthew Olzmann, serves as both Mumford Writer-in-Residence and Citywide Poets co-director, Citywide Poets is an InsideOut afterschool workshop for dedicated high school writers. The workshop's approximately 8 to 12 students are from throughout the Metropolitan Detroit area. They have a strong interest in both writing and performing their poetry. "Our goal is to help facilitate young people's ability to express themselves through writing and related activities," said Olzmann. "The students have a lot of input into what we do…graduates are encouraged to come back and interact with others." Activities include writing exercises, critiques, guest artist sessions and public event performances. The ultimate achievement involves creation of publications showcasing student work including cover art.

Last fall, Citywide Poets opened ArtServe's 18th Annual Governor's Arts Awards. Olzmann reported the group is preparing for several more public appearances including the free Detroit Public Library Main Branch's Java & Jazz Coffee House Series in May.

"As we move into our tenth year, I can only imagine this work getting stronger and better," said InsideOut Director Blackhawk upon acceptance of the Arts Excellence Promoter of the Year Award for 2004 from Alabama A& M University Alumni Association Detroit Renaissance Chapter. Blackhawk is a multi-award winning retired teacher who envisioned InsideOut. She ensures that it maintains standards set while growing up in her North Rosedale Park home before relocating to Woodward Avenue's historic Palms Building. Based on these insights, predictions of the woman who enjoys "the view and family spirit" of her Project's downtown Detroit headquarters are destined to come true.

Everyone is invited to join InsideOut for its 10th Annual Gala at the Gem Theatre/Century Club starting at 6 p.m. on May 25, 2004. This year's theme is "The Power of Poetry: Celebrating 10 Years of Fostering Literary Arts Among Detroit Youth". The special guest speaker is acclaimed poet Nikki Giovanni. Citywide Poets will perform throughout the evening. The festivities will also include private VIP reception, strolling supper, cash bar, fine arts silent auction, video viewing and book signing.

For additional information about InsideOut or to support the Gala through sponsorship/ticket purchases, call (313) 965-5332. You can also visit www.insideoutdetroit.org.

*This article first appeared in **Legacy News** in April 4 – May 1, 2004 issue as part of the Woodward Ambassadors and is reprinted with permission.*

Women Artists Honored

The National Women's History Project (NWHP) has once again selected a thought-provoking theme for celebrating National Women's History Month in March 2008. It is "Women's Art: Women's Vision" and recognizes the distinctive creations of a dozen special women. The honorees' roster includes Judy Chicago (Painter/Printmaker/ Tapestry/ Needlework); Harmony Hammond (Painter); Edna Hibel (Colorist, Painter, Stone Lithographer, Serigrapher, Etcher, Sculptress and Filmmaker); Lihua Lei (Multimedia Installation); Violet Oakley (Muralist, Stained Glass Artist); Rose Cecil O'Neil (Painter, Illustrator, Sculptress); Faith Ringgold (Painter/Quilter), Miriam Schapiro (Print/ Painter); Lorna Simpson (Artist); Juane Quick-To-See Smith (Painter/Printmaker), Nancy Spero (Painter) and June Claire Wayne (Painter/Lithographer). They were chosen based on their art, vision, art form, cultural background and the region in which they live plus the quality and passion of nomination submitted.

"The history of women's art is quintessential women's history," acknowledged NWHP on its Web site. "This year's theme provides a special opportunity to discover and celebrate women's visual arts in a variety of forms and mediums that help expand our perceptions of ourselves and each other." For additional information, visit www.nwhp.org.

"The theme should encourage aspiring artists not to be afraid," stated EENER COLLECTIONS Owner and talented local artist Jarita R. Halliburton.

"If you feel there is something you want to try creatively, go ahead." Halliburton definitely knows dreams can come true. After the death of her husband and children's departure for college, there was a void to fill. Halliburton's pastor encouraged her to allow personal gifts to manifest themselves. Approximately one month later, she dreamed about a beautiful painting then awoke with the strong desire to paint. Her daughter purchased art supplies as a Christmas present. Halliburton has painted approximately 600 original paintings since then.

That is a remarkable achievement for someone who has been an evangelist for approximately 30 years, mother of 4 grown children, grandmother of 6 children and singer/songwriter but never had any artistic inclinations. This was in spite of the fact that she grew up in Minneapolis surrounded by a lot of creative energy from her pastor father and missionary mother who both sang plus 8 siblings forming the Barge Family Singers.

"My relationship with Jesus has sustained me and family members down through the years," Halliburton acknowledged. "I am very happy that this gift of artistic expression was manifest at the right season of my life." Consequentially, she has grown from someone being clueless about art to an artist who enjoys playing with her craft.

"A lot of creative people have a lot of frustration getting things to focus so I would paint the house but not put anything on canvas or paper," Halliburton acknowledged. Now in addition to putting vibrant colors on canvas sometimes reflecting natural themes, she has created a small collection of colored pencil floral etchings. Halliburton revealed that she has a short term goal to have an art show this year and long term goal to be a gallery owner. For additional information about Halliburton or her "Art From The

Heart"-themed business, e-mail atiraj2002@
yahoo.com.

NWHP reminds us that "The
knowledge of women's history provides a
more expansive vision of what a woman can
do. This perspective can encourage girls and
women to think larger and bolder and can
give boys and men a fuller understanding of
the female experience".

*This article first appeared in **Legacy
News** in March 2 – April 5, 2008 issue and
is reprinted with permission.*

Leap Year Baby Still Leaping for Joy

It didn't take long for Ella M. Isom to learn about leap year. The extra day traditionally added every four years, Feb. 29, was her birthday.

"At first, I couldn't understand what it meant not to have a birthday every year," Isom recalled. Ironically, her father was the Sunday School superintendent and made sure other children's birthdays were celebrated regularly. Carrie and Jerry Isom were part of the Niagara Falls, NY New Hope Baptist Church founding group. They taught Isom many valuable lessons she shared during a church history 60th anniversary banquet keynote speech.

"Being religious people, they said 'you don't have to make up a lie: here's the calendar and it shows not having a birthday every year is just the way it is for you," she explained.

Egyptian Pharaoh Ptolemy III. originated the leap year idea. It was first used after Julius Caesar introduced his Julian calendar in 46 B.C. This solar plan had regular years of 365 and one-quarter days plus an odd one every four years.

A Gregorian calendar replaced the Julian one in 1582. It launched the actual expression "leap year" because Pope Gregory XIII., who developed the calendar, decreed that every fourth year would be called by that name – with a few technical exceptions.

Some relationships grew by leaps and bounds on Feb. 29 because romance played an important part in celebrations. Until recent years, many women waited and made marriage proposals during leap year. Some U.S. local governments supported pursuing bachelors then.

Isom discovered one of the advantages for U.S. citizens is that leap year babies can renew their driver's licenses during March. Although some of them celebrate on Feb. 28, she considers March 1 the logical alternative.

The retired social worker and church organist still supports educational institutions and shares musical talents. After being one of a few African American young women in her Niagara Falls high school graduating class, she was encouraged to attend Spelman, a historically Black women's college. World War II. and her father's death meant Isom returned before graduation. Isom was later inspired by Detroit employment opportunity news to move here. She earned her liberal arts degree at Wayne State University because they didn't offer enough classes at night for music majors.

Isom never missed a Spelman reunion and received special honors at one of them. She has served as musician for the Inter Alumni Council UNCF dinner for more than 30 years and the UNCF representative for Sigma Gamma Rho Sorority, Inc. – Rho Sigma Chapter. Isom, who both played by ear and read notes, assists others as People's Community Church's funeral organist.

Isom fondly remembers when Sander's, current makers of hot fudge topping and candy plus previous owners of popular ice cream and sweet shops, gave leap year babies free birthday cakes. What will she wish for before blowing out birthday candles this year?

"I just wish for continued good health and the ability to be self-sufficient with the help of Christ," she revealed. "If that wish comes true, everything else will fall into place."

On Isom's birthday, she may decide to take advantage of another lazy Sunday afternoon.

"I'm young at heart but growing older so I'm still leaping for joy but have almost arrived," she acknowledged with a hearty laugh.

*This article first appeared in **The Michigan FrontPage** March 12, 2004 issue and is reprinted with permission.*

REMARKABLE REPRINTS Online

For a glimpse or long look at photos or illustrations for some of the article and column subjects, visit *REMARKABLE REPRINTS* Online (RRO) via nirmm.wordpress.com. Enjoy viewing the photo portraits and much more.

Other Web highlights include the following resources.

- *REMARKABLE REPRINTS* Updates sharing "where they are now views" with the latest news.

- *REMARKABLE REPRINTS* Revisited Events Calendar featuring book-linked signature series dates and others worthy of marking on your calendar.

REMARKABLE
REPRINTS Revisited

REMARKABLE REPRINTS Revisited
(RRR) is a book-linked signature event series
featuring reunion meet and greets with
contributors/article and column subjects.
Plans call for RRR to include the following
aspects.

- Workshops, seminars, presentations,
  literary events and tours reflecting
  collaborations between *REMARKABLE*
  REPRINTS author/contributors/article
  or column subjects.
- Giveaways and prizes drawings
- Light/theme-linked refreshments

Check periodically for RRR dates listed on the
REMARKABLE REPRINTS Revisited
Events Calendar via nirmm.wordpress.com.

REMARKABLE REPRINTS Feedback and Referral Opportunities

It is the author's hope that reading ***REMARKABLE REPRINTS*** was an enjoyable and enlightening experience for you. Readers can share feedback by e-mailing housereads@yahoo.com with "RR review" in the subject line.

If you have suggestions for future article or column subjects or topics, contact the author by sending e-mail to her at housereads@yahoo.com with "future tips" in the subject line. Thank you for your support. Best wishes for many more remarkable reading experiences.

ABOUT THE AUTHOR

Darlene House is the House of Communications owner and chief communications specialist. She is an award-winning advertising copywriter, editor, journalist, market research expert, marketing specialist and public relations practitioner. House's articles have appeared in academic, mainstream and target market newspapers and magazines throughout her native Metropolitan Detroit area, Southeastern Michigan region, nationally and on the international scene. In addition, she assists authors/poets and non profits with signature event creation and distinctive promotional efforts.

House is a past president of Detroit Working Writers and Women in Communications of Detroit. On the national scene, she originated the National Inspirational Role Models Month (NIRMM) celebration held annually in November Along with many other pioneering efforts, House also originated and launched the Rho Sigma Foundation Sigmas Promoting Inspirational, Resourceful and Insightful Torchbearers (SPIRIT) Awards for "innovative educators" plus NIRMM Literary Leaders Awards.

Send e-mail alerts marked "remarkable idea" to housereads@yahoo.com about event, keynote, conference, workshop or any other opportunities for House's consideration.

www.ingramcontent.com/pod-product-compliance
Lightning Source LLC
Chambersburg PA
CBHW030014290326
41934CB00005B/341